Memories
of
Oxford

Part of the

Memories

series

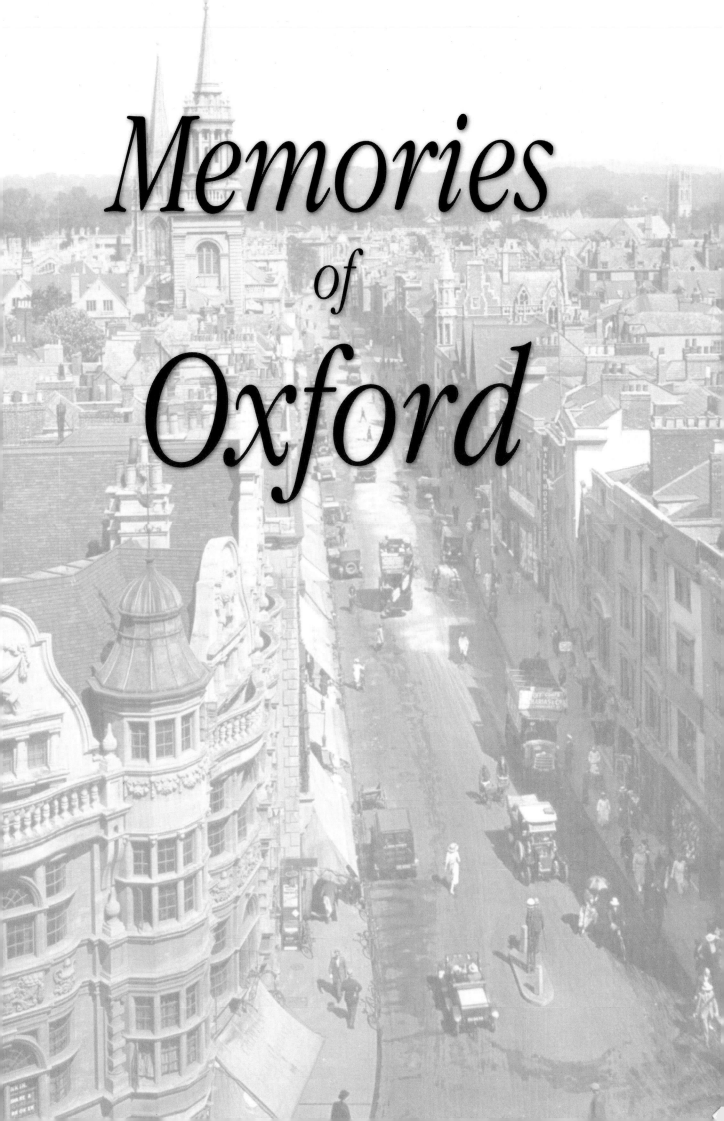

Memories
of
Oxford

*The Publishers would like to thank the following companies for supporting
the production of this book*

Aylesbury Mushrooms Limited

Berkshire,Buckinghamshire and Oxfordshire Wildlife Trust

Edmund Gibbs

Harold Hicks Limited

W Lucy & Company Limited

W G Powell Limited

Wenn Townsend

First published in Great Britain by True North Books Limited
Units 3 - 5 Heathfield Industrial Park
Elland West Yorkshire
HX5 9AE
Tel. 01422 377977
© Copyright: True North Books Limited 1999

ISBN 1 900463 54 7

*Text, design and origination by True North Books Limited
Printed and bound by The Amadeus Press Limited*

Memories are made of this

Memories. We all have them: people, places and events, some good and some bad. Our memories of the place where we grew up are usually tucked away in a very special place in our mind. The best are probably connected with our childhood and youth, when we longed to be grown up and paid no attention to adults who told us to enjoy being young, as these were the best years of our lives. We look back now and realise that they were right.

Old photographs bring our memories flooding back - coronations and celebrations; talking pictures, Technicolour and television; the war years, rationing, and the shared hopes and fears which created such a warm community spirit; buying things made of nylon and plastic; fashions which took trouserbottoms and hemlines from drainpipes and mini-skirts to the other

extreme; Doris Day, Acker Bilk, Elvis Presley and the Beatles; the jitterbug, the tango and discos; Ford Populars and Minis; decimalisation. Life changed so much over the years. Some changes were big, some small; some altered our lives in ways we never anticipated. Who in the early days of motoring could have foreseen the motorways and traffic systems of the latter decades of the 20th century? Did any of us realise, when we first saw a computer, what a tremendous impact they would have on our lives? Self-service supermarkets and frozen food made our lives easier - but at the expense of our friendly little corner shops. Nostalgia is always such a mixture of feelings . . . We hope that the collection of pictures in this book will remind you of happy days in bygone eras - and who knows, you might even have been there when one of the photographs was taken!

Contents

Around the city centre

This shot from High Street, dating from the late 40s or early 50s, captures the historic heart of Oxford in the shape of the Carfax Tower. The first written mention of Oxford goes back as far as 912 AD, and by 1032 St Martin's or Carfax Church stood at these central crossroads. The existing tower was built in the 14th century and served as a focal point for the frequent 'town and gown' riots of medieval times. The scholars accused the townsfolk of charging exorbitant prices for food and rent, whilst the citizens resented the fact that church courts protected students from the consequences of their frequent law-breaking. At the slightest provocation, the sound of the 'Scholar's Bell' ringing at St Mary's, and the answering tones from the city church of St Martin's, would soon turn the area around Carfax into a battlefield. The most bloody incident took place in February 1355, the Massacre of St Scholastica's Day. No less than 63 students were killed (the townsfolk dead remained uncounted), and until 1825 town officials had to pay an annual fine at St Mary's Church. The demolition of St Martin's Church in 1896 was due to road widening, and not part of the penance, but it still left the Carfax Tower as a reminder of those turbulent days.

This is it - the famous skyline which moved Matthew Arnold to describe Oxford as, 'that sweet city with her dreaming spires.' And that skyline remains much the same today as it did at the time of this photograph, 1922. Only a glance downwards at the traffic on High Street gives any sense of era to the shot. The tower at the far left is the Bodleian Tower of the Five Orders, representing the five different styles of classical architecture. The Bodleian Library houses some 5½ million books. An underground tunnel links the old and new Bodleian Libraries, and the Radcliffe Camera. The latter, completed in 1749,

is the domed building to the right of the Bodleian, for which it serves as a reading room and store. More centrally, just to the left of the High Street, the spire of the former All Saints Church stands to the fore of that of St Mary the Virgin. The first tower to the left of High Street is the famous 15th century Bell Tower of Magdalen College, from the summit of which the choir boys sing a Latin hymn each May Day morning. Finally to the tower on the far right, belonging to Merton College, founded in 1264 and boasting the oldest Quad in Oxford, the 14th century Mob Quad.

Above: By 1945 Oxford City Council felt that pressures were building up which could no longer be ignored, the principle one being the growing volume of traffic. Therefore the planning consultant, Thomas Sharp, was asked to prepare a report on the possible future development of the city. The result was 'Oxford Replanned,' a controversial scheme which was accompanied by two large models, one of which is featured in the photograph. Under the direction of Patrick Horsburgh and Brian Crossland, students from the Oxford School of Architecture helped to make the models. The gist of the extract on the wall was the need to stop parked cars cluttering up the heart of Oxford by providing car parks away from the centre, albeit with easy access. Maybe not much argument there, but when Sharp reiterated the need for a relief road running across Christ Church Meadow, to be named Merton Mall, reactions were predictably hostile. It is fascinating to view the model and try to identify the old Oxford alongside the proposed new features. In the event, the radical proposals were never carried through, but in the light of what has happened since the late 1970s it is interesting to look at another of Sharp's conclusions - that Oxford was too dependent on the car industry for employment, and that diversification was necessary.

The decision to restrict private motoring in the centre of Oxford has done much, perhaps thankfully, to make such scenes a thing of the past. The dress and the vehicles on view give an early 1950s flavour to the photograph and the existence of the Clarendon Hotel, with its iron balcony railings, on the left of Cornmarket Street, confirms the rough dating. This fine Oxford landmark was demolished in the mid-50s, amidst much controversy, to build a Woolworth store. In a busy, not to say chaotic scene, admirers of old buses will cast a loving gaze on the two single-deckers approaching the camera, whilst others might appreciate the natty little open-top sports car wedged between them. Nevertheless the shoppers and the bus queues on the crowded pavements were being treated to an unpleasant cocktail of fumes, and matters were only to worsen as the age of mass car ownership began in the 1960s. At this stage, however, you could always nip into the Golden Cross Hotel, featured on the right, for some liquid relief. In the background, across the junctions of St Michael's Street and George Street, the department store of Elliston & Cavell is visible. This was taken over by Debenhams in 1953.

Below: The 99 step climb to the top of Carfax Tower is well worth it to enjoy the view of the High Street. The architectural historian, Pevsner, went so far as to describe it as 'one of the world's great streets.' From that aspect, the modern-day view would differ little from that captured in this 1960s photograph, although restrictions on private vehicles on the High Street have certainly altered the traffic perspective. The prominent building on the immediate left, with its fine carvings, gables and balconies, was designed in 1900-1, and is occupied by the Lloyds TSB Bank. Further along, the first building reaching to the sky is the 18th century All Saints' Church, which became the city church from 1896, when St Martin's at Carfax was demolished. It was closed as a church in 1971. Just behind All Saints', the University Church of St Mary the Virgin is visible, perhaps most famous as being the scene of the heresy trials of Bishops Latimer, Ridley and Cranmer in 1555-56. Famous colleges line both sides of High Street - Brasenose, All Souls, Queen's, St Edmund Hall and Magdalen to the left; Oriel and University to the right. Each has its own unique qualities, although both Daniel Defoe in the 1700s, and much later Pevsner, awarded the accolade of the most beautiful to Queen's.

Right: A busy scene in Cornmarket Street shows some typical 1950s vehicles, but the presence of the rubber block surface indicates that the picture cannot be later than 1955, for that was when the skid-prone surface was taken up. Long ago North Gate Street was the name attached to this highway running from Carfax to the old North Gate of Oxford. St Michael's Tower, visible in the background, stood alongside the North Gate. The gate was demolished in 1771, but the Saxon tower of St Michael's remained, and is the oldest building in the city. The name of the street changed when it became the focal point for trading in corn, and in 1536 a covered arcade was constructed in the middle of the street to keep the sacks dry. This was demolished in 1644, and a Corn Exchange was later built elsewhere. Nevertheless, Cornmarket Street has always had a commercial slant, full of small shops and inns in the 19th century. Between Market Street and Ship Street, for example, there were three inns - the Bell, the White Hart and the Blue Anchor. The 1950s shot features a famous old Cornmarket trading name in the background, 'Zac's for Macs,' but later trends have been towards large stores, banks and fast-food outlets.

If the crossroads at Carfax was the bloody battle-ground on which students and townsfolk met in combat in the Middle Ages, by the 1960s the struggle had transformed itself into one between motor vehicles and pedestrians, with a few bicycles thrown in to irritate both sides. This view of congestion down Cornmarket Street, with its undertones of delay and frustration, would only worsen until the imposition of traffic restrictions in 1971 when the street was closed to most traffic. A quiet battle of a different sort, a financial one, is also taking place at the Carfax junction. Almost 'locking horns' across the street are the Midland Bank (later HSBC), whose old emblem can be seen high on the wall to the left, and Lloyds Bank (later Lloyds TSB). Next to the latter is a shop which proudly displays its watches from Switzerland. The white building much further down on the right, at the street junction, was originally built for Marks & Spencer. The 'Oxford Mail' news vendor is doing brisk trade in the foreground to the left, whilst the well-known Oxford bakery name of Cadena is prominent on the bread van. Shops come and go, and a modern-day stroll down Cornmarket Street would find some new names, including the ubiquitous MacDonalds.

At leisure

> St Giles' Fair still exerts the same magical influence in Oxford today

Separated by 21 years, this photograph and the one overleaf show St Giles' Fair exerting the same magnetic influence on the citizens of Oxford in 1930 as in 1951, and as it still does around half a century on. Swings, roundabouts, stalls, ice-cream, noise and colour - above all some fun and excitement - the appeal is changeless and timeless. The 1930 crowds *(this page)* seem to have regarded it as very much of a 'dressed-up' occasion, for people are generally looking smart in appearance, with a good selection of ladies' hats on display. It was certainly a family occasion as well, although if you were single and 'fancy-free,' it did no harm to be looking your best! That perennial favourite, the roundabout, is doing good business, whilst no doubt the more hair-raising rides produced their regular quota of ear-piercing screams - a good excuse for a young man to clutch a young lady tightly. Dress styles in the 1951 photograph *(overleaf)* seem to be that little less formal, but otherwise the scenario would have been much the same as in 1930. 'The Lion Show,' however, invites some speculation. It may have been one of those spectacles that didn't quite live up to its exciting billing. Perhaps a few Oxonians might remember if that was the case.

Fairs have a long pedigree at Oxford, almost always associated with saints' days - a combination of religious observance, festivities and large-scale trading. One of the earliest was St Benedict's Fair, held as far back as 1122. The great St Giles' Fair, traditionally held in early September, evolved from the parish wake of St Giles, first recorded in 1624. By 1775 mention is made of 'back-sword playing' - an intriguing notion. During the first decades of the 1800s, the fair seems to have been largely for children, with stalls of fruit, gingerbread and toys. By 1838, however, the adults were muscling in, attracted by

dancing booths and the selling of strong drink. Very soon afterwards St Giles' Fair had become a major holiday for the working people of Oxford and the whole county. Strong drink, sharp trading practices and the activities of tricksters, can be a powerful combination. Drunken brawling was not uncommon, so much so that an attempt was made to ban the fair in 1894 because of its 'baneful and injurious influence.' Luckily the attempt failed, for who can forget those days when setting off for the fair meant the quickening of both pulse and footsteps at the sound of the music and the sight of the bright lights against the night sky?

A myriad of thoughts can occupy the mind of a young boy sitting on a park bench. Perhaps he is watching the changing pattern of shadows created by his feet as the sun slants across. Perhaps he is imagining that the ground is alive with monsters, and only keeping his feet off the ground will ensure his safety. Or, more prosaically, maybe he has just got fed up of sitting by himself, and is about to go off and seek some company. This little study was captured in Oatlands Road recreation ground around 1930. Those whose recollections of childhood reach back beyond 1950 or so will appreciate how different life was then for children - no televisions, no videos, no computers. The streets were full of children 'playing out,' creating their own games in a world that was largely free of adult supervision. Football, cricket, hop-scotch, skipping, marbles, hide-and-seek, conkers, cigarette card trading - just some of the ingredients of a child's outdoor world. If it was wet, then it was the turn of the indoor games such as cards, ludo, snakes and ladders, lotto and bagatelle. Were we any worse off for not having all the modern electronic 'goodies'? Probably not, but there is no doubt of what we would have done had they been offered to us!

Above: Three smart lads pose for the camera in this picture from the late 1950s, bringing memories of our school days flooding back. The first thing to strike us is just how smart the little lads were, despite the fact that money was tight and it was not always easy to find cash to spend on clothing. Still, people did the best with what they had, homemade haircuts and hand-me-down clothes made up for the lack of money when the need arose. The picture highlights just how much fashions have changed since the era featured here. Try getting your little lad to wear short trousers and white ankle socks... let alone a tie!

Top: The ice rink which opened on Botley Road in 1930 had a solid if rather uninspiring frontage. Nevertheless it hoped to achieve success because of Oxford's tradition of skating. Hard winters in the past had seen skaters out on the River Cherwell, or even the Thames, but more often on the frozen surfaces of flooded meadows, such as Port Meadow. The indoor rink held daily sessions, accompanied by Max Chappell's orchestra. Special events included guest figure skaters and barrel jumpers, along with ice hockey matches. In November 1930, for example, Oxford University defeated Germany 3-1. The photograph of the rink gives some idea of its great size, but running costs were high and attendances fell below expectations. In the summer of 1933 it was converted to a cinema, and after one more winter of ice skating, it remained a cinema. The Majestic Theatre opened in April 1934, and with a 2,500 seating capacity the owners perhaps could rightly boost that it was, 'the largest picture theatre in the South Midlands.' Mae West's 'I'm No Angel' opened the first programme. The life of the Majestic was fairly short-lived, for by 1947 Frank Cooper's 'Oxford Marmalade' was established in the building. Indoor ice skating returned to Oxford in 1984, with the opening of a new rink at Oxpens Road.

The ex-coal barge, 'Gertrude,' is seen here at Duke's Lock, at the far end of a delightful return trip on the evening of June 29th 1961. The lucky trippers were members of the Oxford City Council Highways and Planning Committee, along with consorts, and they had set off at around 6pm from Hythe Bridge. The calm and tranquil nature of the evening was no doubt enhanced by the fact that 'Gertrude' was pulled by a horse. From time to time the Mayor, Alderman Harrison, took the tiller as the passengers enjoyed the views in general, but particularly those of the gardens of many North

Oxford houses. The organiser and benefactor was Mr Ferguson, a former council member, who wished to entertain some of his ex-colleagues. This he did generously, with 'ploughman's lunch' type fare, and plenty of sherry. The goodwill gesture was not entirely altruistic, for Mr Ferguson was also seeking to provide practical evidence for one of his pet schemes - a relief highway to the Woodstock and Banbury roads along the line of the canal. The evening jaunt was partly an attempt to show councillors how easy this would be whilst, perhaps, putting them in a mellow mood.

Wartime

In 1939 Britain's Prime Minister Neville Chamberlain had made his announcement to the waiting people of Britain that '...this country is at war with Germany.' The country rolled up its sleeves and prepared for the inevitable. This war would be different from other wars. This time planes had the ability to fly further and carry a heavier load, and air raids were fully expected. Air raid shelters were obviously going to be needed, and shelters were built on open places across the town.

By the time war was declared an army of volunteers of both sexes had already been recruited to form an Air Raid Protection service. At first ARP personnel were unpaid volunteers but when war broke out in September 1939 they became paid staff. It was their job to patrol specified areas, making sure that no chinks of light broke the blackout restrictions, checking the safety of local residents, being alert for gas attacks, air raids and unexploded bombs. The exceptional work done by Air Raid Wardens in dealing with incendiaries, giving first aid to the injured, helping to rescue victims from their bombed-out properties, clearing away rubble, and a thousand and one other tasks became legendary; during the second world war nearly as many private citizens were killed as troops - and many of them were the gallant ARP wardens.

In May 1940 Anthony Eden, Secretary of State for War, appealed in a radio broadcast for men between 17 and 65 to make up a new force, the Local Defence Volunteers, to guard vulnerable points from possible Nazi attack. Within a very short time the first men were putting their names down. At first the new force had to improvise; there were no weapons to spare and men had to rely on sticks, shotguns handed in by local people, and on sheer determination . Weapons and uniforms did not become available for several months.

In July the Local Defence Volunteers was renamed the Home Guard, and by the following year were a force to be reckoned with. Television programmes such as 'Dad's Army' have unfortunately associated the Home Guard with comedy, but in fact they performed much important work. The Guard posted sentries to watch for possible aircraft or parachute landings at likely spots such as disused aerodromes, golf courses on the outskirts of towns, local parks and racecourses. They manned anti-aircraft rocket guns, liaised with other units and with regular troops, set up communications and organised balloon barrages.

Other preparations were hastily made around the town. Place names and other identifying marks were obliterated to confuse the enemy about exactly where they were. Notices went up everywhere giving good advice to citizens on a number of issues. 'Keep Mum - she's not so dumb' warned people to take care what kind of information they passed on, as the person they were speaking to could be an enemy.

Older readers will remember how difficult it was to find certain items in the shops during the war; combs, soap, cosmetics, hairgrips, elastic, buttons, zips - all were virtually impossible to buy as factories that once produced these items had been turned over to war work. Stockings were in short supply, and resourceful women resorted to colouring their legs with gravy browning or with a mixture of sand and water. Beetroot juice was found to be a good substitute for lipstick.

Clothes rationing was introduced in 1941, and everyone had 66 coupons per year. Eleven coupons would buy a dress, and sixteen were needed for a coat. The number of coupons was later reduced to 40 per person. People were required to save material where they could - ladies' hemlines went up considerably, and skirts were not allowed to have lots of pleats. Some found clever ways around the regulations by using materials that were not rationed. Blackout material could be embroidered and made into blouses or skirts, and dyed sugar sacks were turned into curtains.

Above: War had been declared, and every citizen of Britain, young and old, male and female, was called upon to put his or her back into the war effort. Those who did not go into military service of one kind or another worked in factories, dug for victory, gave up their aluminium baths and saucepans, joined organisations and aided in any way they could. These boys were not going to be left out; they might be too young to fight but while there were sandbags to be filled they were going to do their bit to protect their school building. Thousands of sandbags were used during World War II to protect the country and its beautiful civic buildings.

Left: A proud father poses for the camera with his latest arrival. The baby had not arrived from Mars, in fact the 'arrival' was not a baby at all, but an anti-gas attack suit which was compulsory for babies in the United Kingdom during the second world war. An air pump at the side of the suit enabled anxious parents to replenish the supply of air to the precious package inside. It is said that most babies were less than enthusiastic abut the prospect of being encased in the suit - and who could blame them? The picture was taken in 1939. In the event there was never any gas attack on British soil during the course of the second world war.

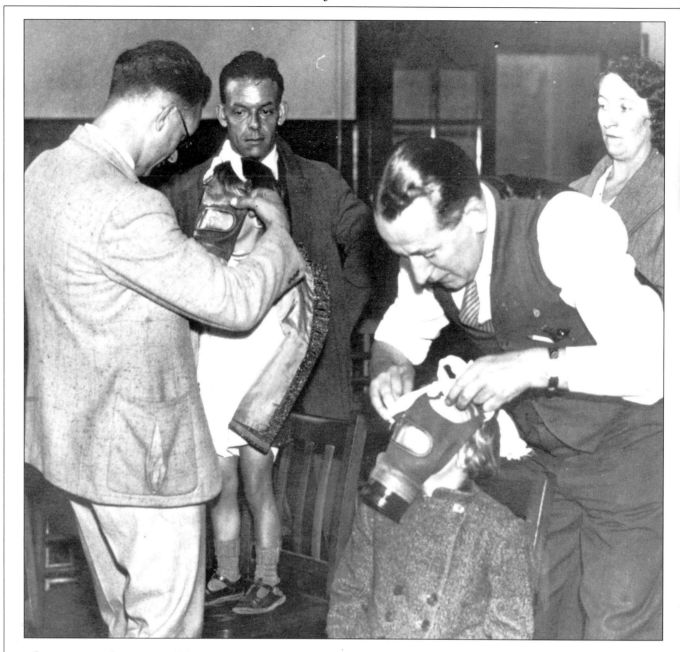

Above: It must have seemed like a nightmare prospect for these Oxford parents as they watched their children being fitted with gas masks in the early days of World War II. And indeed, 'nightmare' was the key word to describe the fears of the government of the possible consequences of large-scale aerial gas attacks. Countrywide the government distributed 38 million gas masks, and 95,000 of these were allocated to Oxford. People were supposed to go nowhere without their gas masks. Gas decontamination squads were set up in Oxford, along with decontamination centres. Terrifying if necessary instructions were sent to house-holders as to how to behave in the event of a gas attack. Contaminated food and clothing had to be destroyed. Ointment was available from chemists to apply to any skin affected by blister gas. The sound of the air raid warden's rattle was to act as both the alert for a gas bomb attack and the all-clear. The difficulty of persuading children not only to don, but to keep on gas masks, was overcome by producing colourful Micky Mouse respirators with tongues hanging out. Older Oxonians may well remember these, along with gas mask practices at school and how, after the gas attacks never came, gas mask boxes were converted into handy lunch boxes.

Right: Could it really be true? There is no mistaking the sense of urgency on the face of the newspaper vendor as he hurries from Newspaper House with his special edition of the 'Oxford Mail.' The date was September 3rd 1939 and the Prime Minister, Neville Chamberlain, had just made his solemn radio announcement that Britain had declared war on Germany in the face of the latter's attack on Poland. Rarely can this newspaper seller have carried headlines that meant so much to both the people of Oxford and the country at large. He was inundated with custom that day. Motorists were even stopping their cars to buy a newspaper. And yet, a sense of disbelief hung in the air. Only twelve months earlier Chamberlain had been saying how unbelievable it was that British people should be digging trenches and trying on gas masks because of the Czechoslovakian crisis. He had described it as a quarrel between people 'of whom we know nothing.' How was the Polish crisis any different? No matter how much people may have been reasoning in this way, the authorities were grimly preparing for the worst. In April 1939 the Chief Constable, C R Fox, had been appointed Air Raid Precaution Controller for Oxford, with a control centre under the Town Hall.

Left: The painful reality of total war is encapsulated in this image of a young evacuee emerging from Oxford station, his sister clutching his hand, in September 1939. The sight of hundreds of such children, mainly from London, carrying their belongings and their gas masks, must have brought home to many Oxonians that the impact of war on civilians could mean considerably more than the inconvenience of the black-out. Reluctant as people had been to face up to the prospect of war, many heeded the call to get their children out of the danger areas, and the first evacuation wave took place on September 1st 1939. By September 6th, 19,830 official evacuees had arrived in Oxford and Oxfordshire. Last-minute changes of plans, along with some confusion as to destinations, caused nightmares for local billeting officers, and emergency accommodation at some of the Oxford colleges had to be utilised. The period of the 'phoney war' tempted many London parents to bring their children back home, but the start of the Blitz there, in September 1940, caused a second influx of evacuees into Oxford. As with elsewhere, the experiences of the evacuees ranged from enjoying generous hospitality to suffering heartless exploitation. For the majority, however, the government slogan of, 'Keep them happy, keep them safe,' was achieved.

Below: 'The day war broke out ....' Many people still remember Rob Wilton's humorous monologue about the typically understated British response to the outbreak of hostilities with Germany. Nevertheless the sight of a policeman in a gas mask giving directions on Queen Street must have convinced a few Oxonians that something serious was afoot, even if the lady looks cheerful enough. If that were not enough, the message concerning black-out material carried by the Starlings sandwichboard man may have convinced a few more. The black-out, imposed nationally so as to deprive German bombers of easy targets, was the first of the many inconveniences of war felt in Oxford. Confusion had reigned on September 1st 1939 when, as a trial, street lighting had been drastically reduced along main roads. Motorists, cyclists and pedestrians all accused each other of selfishness, whilst special constables had difficulty making their authority felt. Gallons of white paint were soon being expended on marking out kerbs, lamp-posts and even trees on streets. The air raid warden's cry of, 'Put that light out,' quickly became a familiar one. All homes, workplaces and public buildings had to be blacked-out, and the number of offenders who were soon appearing in court shows just how stringently the authorities enforced the regulations.

'*The bomber will always get through*' *stated Prime Minister Stanley Baldwin in 1936*

These workers at Windmill Road, Headington, have plenty of interested spectators as they construct an air raid shelter in 1939. 'The bomber will always get through,' had stated Prime Minister Stanley Baldwin in 1936, and it was with this air of fatalism that the government awaited massive casualties in the first months of the war. Nevertheless air raid precautions went on apace, and by 1939 Oxford had 1337 volunteer wardens manning 70 wardens' posts. Ambulance stations, first aid posts, auxiliary fire stations and emergency water supplies were put in a state of readiness. Central Oxford had some large-scale public air raid shelters, including refuges beneath Balliol College, Christ Church and the covered market. By 1942, the lowest basement of the New Bodleian Library had been converted into a shelter for up to 1100 people. The original contents - 2000 of the Library's greatest treasures - were packed off to a deep stone quarry near Bath. Street shelters were constructed in Oxford's suburbs, along with others at schools and factories. People could even buy their own private household versions in the shape of Anderson and Morrison Shelters. Incredibly, in spite of all the vital war-work going on at Cowley, only one bomb fell on Oxford during the war - harmlessly between Littlemore and Cowley.

Left: An absolutely immaculate array of kit is laid out for inspection in Hut 34 of Cowley Barracks in July 1941. Everything is neat and precise, according to regulations, with the handle of the mug at right-angles to the bed, and the badge on the cap facing straight ahead. Even the suitcase and helmet on top of the cupboard seem to be sitting at attention. How long all this took only an ex-servicewoman (or man) would know, but it is to be hoped that some slight error did not provoke the inspecting officer to tip the lot off the bed, causing the poor ATS girl to start all over again! She stands 'at ease,' looking very smart, but she was probably somewhat tense within. Could that mat be an inch out of place? The ATS was the Auxiliary Territorial Service, a support group for the Army, and other women's units acted in a similar capacity for the Navy and the Air Force. War does bring about social change, and World War I had brought women into munitions factories or into 'men's' jobs because of the demands on manpower for the front line. However, by the time of World War II many women were in uniform, and more closely involved in the military side of things.

Below: Economy was the watchword in the Britain of World War II, and where it couldn't be imposed by rationing, the government had to rely upon persuasion. This impressive exhibition concentrated on water and fuel, giving a host of hints as to how to save both. Oddly, with the exception of the fire-poking instructions, many of the appeals have a contemporary air about them. Modern environmentalists would greatly approve of lagging a hot water boiler. And who can forget the drought of 1995, and the desperate appeals for water conservation? However, although some water boards suggested that people bathed less frequently, at least it wasn't recommended that they used only five inches of water! There was one big difference between modern-day conservation campaigns and those of the war years. The latter were aimed at the defeat of the man portrayed in the middle - Hitler. Wartime Britain became a land of slogans - 'Waste not Want not,' 'Make do and Mend,' 'Dig for Victory.' Resources, especially food, were scarce. Industry had to concentrate on the war effort and so there were great salvage campaigns for paper, glass and metal. Money saved could be invested in war savings, with the aim of defeating Hitler. The most powerful image was that of the swastika decorated Squander Bug, reminding people of the dangers of waste.

Army camps and airfields were thick on the ground throughout Oxfordshire

The Oxford of 'town and gown' was transferred into the Oxford of gown and kitbag during World War II. It is doubtful whether the two soldiers even cast a glance at the two female undergraduates, even to admire their immaculately straight-seamed stockings, so familiar had the one become to the other. The size of the Territorial Army had to be doubled after 1939, and at Cowley the regimental depot of the Oxfordshire and Buckinghamshire Light Infantry became an Infantry Training Centre. It was unable to accommodate the pressure of numbers, and by early 1940 Slade Camp had been set up on a field between Brasenose Wood and Open Magdalen Wood. The Examination Schools were requisitioned for use as a military hospital, and St Hugh's College had a similar role, but specialising in head injuries. Army camps and airfields were thick on the ground throughout Oxfordshire, and it was decided that the county's terrain was ideal for tank exercises. Exercise Spartan, in March 1943, saw a convoy of Bren gun carriers rumbling along Beaumont Street. Many servicemen and women were attracted into Oxford in their off-duty hours, and the YMCA converted the Carfax Assembly Rooms into a forces canteen, with leisure facilities attached. Forces personnel also enjoyed free admittance to the Bodleian Library.

Both pictures: *The image of 'Dad's Army' is a difficult one to dispel whenever mention is made of the Home Guard, and the accounts of those who served tend to emphasise the ludicrous and the incompetent. Nevertheless the broadcast appeal on May 14th 1940 of Anthony Eden, the Secretary of State for War, for the formation of a force to defend Britain from invasion, was made with serious intent. The Local Defence Volunteers (renamed the Home Guard in July 1940) had a prime role of defending strategic points against parachutists - gasworks, road and railway bridges, water towers etc. Initial problems included lack of training and weapons. Clubs, knives, primitive pikes, ancient shotguns - these were some of the weapons with which the LDV prepared to face trained enemy soldiers. Also, the demands of conscription meant that the force was composed of those who were too young, too old or too unfit for active military service. At least the Oxford contingent had more than its share of brain power. For example Dr C M Bowra, Warden of Wadham, was a lieutenant, and Lord Elton became a sergeant. Nevertheless cynics were not convinced that German parachutists could be repelled by the power of the intellect alone, and claimed that LDV stood for, 'Look, Duck and Vanish,' or 'Long Dentured Veterans'!*

Both photographs suggest a predominance of older soldiers in the Home Guard, but they also suggest a force that has gone well beyond the 'drilling with walking sticks' stage. The first essential of proper weaponry was soon being met by the arrival of rifles from the USA, to be supplemented by Lewis guns, Browning automatics and Sten guns. Training was the next essential, and shooting practice (shown above) for Oxford companies took place at Cowley Barracks and Slade Camp among other places. Live bomb throwing was carried out on a battalion range in Old Road. Field exercises with regular troops helped to instil some professionalism, although tempers could become frayed when participants refused to accept that they had been 'shot'! The Abingdon Company held a successful training camp at Sutton Courtenay in August 1941, whilst in Oxford an assault course was opened in Jackdaw Lane in 1942. It was measures such as these which turned the Home Guard into the smart outfit shown in the second photograph (right), swinging (almost) in step together past The Plain as part of a large parade. 'D'-Day and the invasion of France finally put paid to any serious threat of a German attack, and the Home Guard was 'stood down' in November 1944.

'All the world loves a parade,' as the saying goes, and a large crowd has gathered to watch this smart body of men go swinging past The Plain, preceded by the bandsmen. The scene took place during World War II, but the exact occasion is uncertain. It may have been a 1945 Victory Parade, or it may have been one of the marches that took place as publicity events for the various fund-raising drives that went on throughout the war. Fighting wars is a costly business, and one way for the government to raise money was by persuading people to buy war bonds of various kinds. Great war savings drives were

inaugurated, the first one at Oxford being War Weapons Week in December 1940. The target was to raise £500,000, the cost of 25 bombers. Various events were put on, including members of the public paying 6d (2½p) each to inspect a Junkers bomber that had been shot down near Blewbury. Large donations from Lord Nuffield, Pressed Steel and the University and colleges helped to swell the total to £1,208,268. Later major drives in Oxford included Worship Week (1941-2), Tanks for Attack Campaign (1942), Wings for Victory Week (1943) and Salute the Soldier Week (1944).

Above: Wars generally tend to turn things upside down, and this photograph is a case in point. The cricket pavilion of Jesus College was built as a domain for men, but by late 1940 it had become a day nursery for children, exclusively staffed by volunteer women. A problem had arisen because the huge demands made on the economy to fight total war against Germany meant that many thousands of women were being asked to leave their homes and enter the workplace, partly to replace conscripted men. Women were employed as sorters and postwomen by the Post Office. They became drivers and conductresses on buses and 'portresses' on railway stations. Most demanding of all, perhaps, was the work done at Cowley, where the Morris Motors factories had been turned into a huge concern for producing war materials. This was all very well, but who was to look after the children? By November 1940 the Ministry of Labour had conceded the necessity of establishing a day nursery in Oxford and it covered the full cost of the featured nursery. In April 1942 a crêche for the children of Cowley workers was opened by Lord Nuffield at the Crescent Road sports ground, the eighth in Oxford. By the end of 1943, there were places for over 500 children in Oxford.

Above right: Both women and men labour away on the assembly line of the Torpedo Shop at Cowley in 1944. Soon after the outbreak of World War II, the factories at Cowley that had produced Morris vehicles, along with those of the Pressed Steel Company, were converted to producing war materials on a massive scale. Working seven day weeks, on shifts that lasted from 8am to 10pm, workers raised output to around 2½ times pre-war levels.

These efforts produced an impressive list of weapons and ancillary products including aerial and naval torpedoes, 'Tiger Moth' aeroplanes, 'Crusader' tanks, sea mines, depth charges, machine-gun tripods, searchlights and wirelesses. Statistics are equally arresting - 6 million ammunition boxes, 3½ million steel helmets, and 2 million jerrycans. Cowley was the headquarters of the Civilian Repair Organisation, organising units nationwide which, over the course of the war, repaired around 80,000 aircraft. Similarly, Cowley housed a salvage organisation which worked nationwide to collect and deliver crashed aircraft to repair workshops. Many came to Cowley, so much so that mounds of broken planes covered 100 acres of farmland. There has been much debate as to why Oxford was not more heavily bombed during the war. One suggestion is that Hitler wanted it intact as his communications centre after the invasion!

Events & occasions

At first sight this could be mistaken for a scene from a Marx brothers film, with Groucho explaining the purpose of the weird barrow, whilst the young man holding the handles stares in frozen disbelief. In truth, this was an inter-war trade fair at which the Cowley engineering firm of John Allen & Sons was exhibiting, amongst other things, the roadless barrow. Caterpillar tracks allowed it to negotiate fields and rough land. The firm had a reputation for ingenious agricultural machinery, although the hefty roller in the background, with the Allen emblem and the ox of Oxford, looks straightforward enough. The onset of World War II saw John Allen continue to produce motor scythes and trenchers, for increased output in agriculture was considered essential if Britain was to be fed during the 'U'-boat campaign against merchant ships. Nevertheless the firm did diversify into products with a more direct military bearing. 'The Rabbit' and 'The Ferret' were somewhat ambitious devices which were intended to breech German defences. However, the concept was ahead of the technology of the time, and these were abandoned. More successful was a range of John Allen products which included machine-gun mountings, anti-mine tank flails, rocket-firing apparatus, and Sheepsfoot rollers for use in the construction of roads and airfields.

May 6th 1935 saw the Silver Jubilee of King George V and Queen Mary. It had been a turbulent 25 years since the Coronation of 1910, a span that had seen the violence of the suffragettes, the horrors of World War I, heavy fighting in Ireland, the General Strike of 1926 and the economic depression of the 'hungry 30's.' Loyalty to the crown, however, had remained largely undiminished, and the people of the country were happy to celebrate what they

perhaps regarded as a rock of stability in an uncertain world. An impressive array of Union Jacks, including one huge one, drapes the interior of what may be a school or a Sunday School at Bath Street, St Clement's. 'Fight the good fight,' proclaims the blackboard, but perhaps this was being postponed for a day as the children sit down to a tea-party. There are fancy hats in abundance as everyone settles down to the message of this particular day - enjoyment.

Above: The focal point of the Silver Jubilee celebrations was, naturally enough, London. There were tumultuous scenes as the royal procession made its way through the streets to St Paul's Cathedral. Among the thousands lining the streets were quite a number from Oxford, for hundreds of people had crowded the early morning trains to London, and a special leaving at 7am had been packed to the doors. Nevertheless there were plenty left behind to ensure that Oxford experienced a truly memorable day. A solemn thanksgiving service was held in the Cathedral Chapel at Christ Church, preceded by a river of scarlet and black as a slow procession of civic and University dignitaries made its way across Tom Quad towards the chapel. Later that morning a commemorative oak tree was planted in the churchyard of St Mary Magdalene, watched by a large crowd. Supplies of flags and bunting for street decorations had been sold out, and it was commented by the 'Oxford Mail' that some of the suburban side streets were more heavily decorated than those of the city centre. This may well have applied to Jericho Street, where a real effort must have gone into the decorating. A packed street tea-party is about to commence, and although everyone else has a 1930s look about them, the youth at the front is strangely 1950s in appearance!

Over at Catherine Street on May 6th 1935, balloons and home-made party hats are the order of the day, but apart from the single flag, the residents don't seem to have gone in for much street decorating. However, a party is in the offing, and it looks as if two long benches have been hauled into position for the group photo-graph. Somehow the person behind the camera hasn't quite got the cheery smiles he or she might have been hoping for. In fact not a little glumness is evident. Perhaps the kids just wanted to get on with the jelly and ice-cream! Events of this nature were taking place all over the city's suburbs,

whilst the centre hosted a number of public ceremonies. The British Legion held a great march to a rally and service at the University Parks. Proudly wearing their medals from a conflict that may have seemed not too far distant in their minds, the members of the Legion gathered before a distinguished platform party which included the Duke of Marlborough. Another notable event was the firing of a 21 round royal salute at midday in the Long Walk, Christ Church Meadow, watched by a large crowd. Four guns of the Royal Artillery did the honours, this being the first royal salute fired in Oxford since 1660.

"SO THE POOR DOG H

Across the city the Jubilee celebrations took a multitude of different forms

Across the city, festivities took a multitude of different forms. The people of Headington Quarry attended an open-air service held on the recreation ground. Meanwhile there were boating parties on the Cherwell, and at Keble College eight red, white and blue rugby shirts formed a patriotic chain between two windows. Moving from one extreme of society to the other, the men at the Salvation Army Hostel were given a special Jubilee dinner. Mrs Scroggs of Oxford Street, Woodstock, gave birth on the afternoon of May 6th, and the baby girl thus qualified to receive a special silver spoon that the 'Oxford Mail' was presenting to all its readers' offspring making their arrivals between May 5th and May 12th. The spoons were solid silver, with a special 1935 hall-mark. Surely some of these still exist as treasured heirlooms. Perhaps too, older Oxonians might have their memories rekindled by these images of May 1935, and may even recognise themselves from that far-off time. Those who lived at Cranham Street, Jericho, for example posed beneath a wonderful advertisement for HP Sauce - an evocative picture indeed.

Howard Street certainly went in for quantity in its celebration of the Silver Jubilee, for a small army looks to have assembled on the grass. The picture is a reminder of what such occasions can do for community spirit, with groups of people combining to organise games, parties and gifts for the children. As the long, sunny day faded into evening, further evidence of this was provided as fairy lights came on in Morrell Avenue, Freelands Road and Wellington Street. Many people crowded into the city centre to look at the floodlighting, and the streets were packed with vehicles and pedestrians. Tom Tower, Magdalen

Bridge and the thousands of red, white and blue lights at St Giles proved to be special attractions, although by general consent the Ashmolean Museum took the unofficial prize. The crowds were so dense that it was taking two hours for buses to get from Iffley Turn to Carfax. As always there was plenty of exuberant behaviour from undergraduates. Around the city fires blazed in the night. North Hinksey lit a huge bonfire, and at nearby Shotover Hill the local Boy Scouts' Association lit a giant beacon which could be seen for miles. The scouts and around 4,000 sightseers sang well into the night.

Above: *Everybody has linked arms and it's a good show of camaraderie at the Christmas 1944 staff party at Starlings. This firm had shops at St Ebbe's Street and Pembroke Street, its retail line being floor covering and household furnishings. It is noticeable that the traditional Christmas decorations have almost been supplanted by union jacks. No doubt this was partly through patriotism, but probably also because of shortages of paper decorations. This was one of the key words of World War II in Britain - 'shortages' - closely followed by 'rationing.' As industry switched to war production, and German 'U'-boats played havoc with merchant ships, rationing was introduced from 1940 on food, fuel, clothing and a whole range of goods. Ration books were issued, and coupons were necessary in order to buy a person's weekly allowances, for example 2 ounces (50g) each of tea, butter and cheese, 4 ounces (100g) of bacon or ham. As for eggs, you were allowed one per fortnight! Britain entered the world of dried eggs, dried milk and spam (spiced ham) from the USA. Oranges and bananas were almost unobtainable luxuries. Nevertheless 'spivs' could get you almost anything on the 'black market' - at a price. So, just how well the Starlings' staff celebrated Christmas 1944 may have depended on just who they knew.*

Right: *There is an interesting range of expressions to be seen on board this packed Salters steamer, ranging from the cheerful, through the indifferent, down to the downright hostile. Perhaps those who looked less than happy were of a pessimistic nature, fearing that a cruise on the River Thames might carry the risk of a 'U'-boat attack, for this was wartime after all! None the less, these passengers deserved a break of some sort, for being members of the Amalgamated Engineers' Union, they and their families were playing a leading part in the war effort at home. Employed at such places as Morris Motors or Pressed Steel at Cowley, both converted to war production, men and women were working long shifts in order to produce such things as tanks, planes, torpedoes and ammunition boxes. It is possible too that this steamer trip was an attempt to compensate workers for the fact that even in their holidays it was difficult to get away to the seaside. A shortage of both petrol and transport saw to that. In July 1943 the Oxford City Council ran a six week 'Holidays at Home' programme. This included donkey rides at Cutteslowe, paddle boats at Hinksey Park, a fun fair at Botley Road and a gala week at Florence Park.*

It is said the walls and quadrangles of Oxford colleges muffle almost all sound from the streets outside, so that the dons and under-graduates can pursue their browsings and meditations in tranquillity. Until very recently the roar and rumble of motorised traffic along High Street has put this to the test, but still relative peace and quiet has reigned within. Perhaps, however, even the innermost rooms of Oriel and Brasenose were penetrated by the unaccustomed but stirring sounds of this Pressed Steel brass band as it led a police parade up The High in 1952. Many people have paused to appreciate the spectacle, for parades have a magnetic appeal, and the leopard skin cape of the big bass drummer is particularly eye-catching. Just as impressive is the way the precision of the march has been caught, as the right foot of each man is about to rise to the beat of that drum. The police were parading close to the 19th century headquarters of the old Oxford City Police, Kemp Hall, a building dating back to 1637. Another venerable building, the Mitre Inn, is visible on the photo-graph. As well as an old frontage, its 13th century cellars stretch half-way across the street, and deep below it.

The headquarters of the old Oxford City Police, Kemp Hall, dated back to 1637

Below centre: Royal events came thick and fast after the Silver Jubilee of King George V and Queen Mary in 1935. First there was the death of the King and the accession of Edward VIII, only to be followed in 1936 by the sensational abdication of the new King, who chose to follow this course of action rather than sever his relationship with the American divorcee, Mrs Wallis Simpson. However, there seems to have been no shortage of enthusiasm for celebrating the Coronation of King George VI on May 12th 1937. Perhaps people saw this as an event which would inaugurate more settled times for the monarchy, and perhaps for the country as a whole. The 'Daily Mail' was offering a tempting £5,000 in prizes in a nationwide shop window display competition to mark the event, and this was the commendable effort of Stevens & Co of Oxford, trading as 'Stevco.' The shop window is a nice mix of patriotism and commercialism, and the discounts are neatly described as making for 'cellar filling prices.' This was a time, of course, when coal was dominant as a domestic fuel. The great day itself, May 12th, proved to be rainy, but a floodlit city centre attracted huge crowds. Elsewhere South Park, Headington, staged a spectacular fireworks display, and numerous street parties were held.

Bottom: Queen Elizabeth II had not quite reached the end of a busy day when this photograph was taken during her 'flying' visit on May 2nd 1968. She is pictured with Dr C A Simpson, the Dean of Christ Church, as she officially opens the new quadrangle behind Blue Boar Street. At the same time, a new picture gallery was opened to the public, displaying some of the college's famous art treasures. Her Majesty's day had begun with a visit to St Ebbe's, where she was shown models and plans for the Westgate development. Shortly afterwards, accompanied by the Mayor, Alderman Frank Pickstock, she was able to examine some of the evidence of Medieval Oxford that the demolitions occasioned by the Westgate project were allowing archaeologists to unearth. With little time to spare, the Queen was then off to North Oxford to lay the foundation stone of the new Wolfson College, the largest resident graduate college in the country. Somerville was the next stop, then Christ Church, before she arrived at Oriel College, the home of the Vice-Chancellor, where she dined. Before leaving Oxford by train, she had just time to listen to the first half-hour of a debate at the Union. All in a day's work!

The annual City Police Church Parade is featured on this photograph and the one overleaf, both from the 1960s. It's a smart 'eyes left' for the Lord Mayor on the first one (above), who has taken up an elevated position opposite the junction with Speedwell Street. The uniformed and top-hatted Lord Mayor's sergeant is visible to the right, mace over his shoulder. Some very fine architecture is to be seen, and for a change the motorists have a chance to examine it, for the cars have slowed down to a very respectful pace behind the procession proceeding down St Aldate's. Hardly surprising considering whom they are following!

Similarly on the second photograph (overleaf), a little further down the street, the 'No Waiting' sign has been strictly adhered to. It is likely that the parade was returning to the police station further down St Aldate's along a route with rich historical associations. St Aldate's was only named as such in the 19th century, in token of the 'old gate' through which travellers had passed to and from the 'oxenforde' at present day Folly Bridge. From 1342 the street had been known as Fish Street, the northern part having hosted a fish market for many centuries, and the old South Gate had stood in the Christ Church area.

SILVER'S
MEN & BOYS
TAILORING &
OUTFITTING

POLICE
NO
WAITING

St Aldate's Central Police Station was set up in 1938 to replace the one which had been earlier established on Blue Boar Street. The Oxford Police Act of 1868 had created a united city police force. Early working conditions were hard, and a constable had to complete his long duty shift without returning to the station unless accompanied by a prisoner or with something to report. In a city full of lively undergraduates, Oxford policemen have often had to make the difficult decision between indulgence towards a student 'prank' or the pressing of charges. November 5th must have been a

The Oxford Police Act of 1868 created a united city police force

nightmare evening. For many years it was traditional for students to try and pinch a policeman's helmet. Matters worsened in the 1960s when both local hooligans and students used the evening as an excuse to run wild. Oxford's growing traffic problem was well underway by the 1960s and the police operated eight manual traffic points at the evening rush hour. One of these was at the junction of Speedwell Street and St Aldate's, and from the nearby police station Chief Constable Burrows could personally keep an eye on proceedings. In 1968, exactly a century after its formation, the Oxford City Police Force lost its independence when it merged with surrounding forces.

On the move

In medieval times Cornmarket Street was paved with cobblestones. The road sloped down to the middle, where there was a gutter or kennel. In the 18th century the street was paved, and from 1881 tram lines ran down the centre. Of all the various surfaces experienced by Cornmarket Street, it is doubtful if there has been a stranger one than the rubber road laid in 1937. The photograph shows workmen putting the finishing touches to one section of what was an interesting experiment. The theory behind it was that the increasing volume of motor traffic was producing such vibration that there was a risk of damage to buildings.

Hence rubber blocks were laid. The practical outcome was a surface which provided no grip in wet weather and often resulted in dangerous skidding. Consequently the rubber blocks were taken up in 1955. The interested little crowd of the photograph is a reminder that at one time watching workmen, particularly digging holes, was a 'spectator sport.' It was especially beloved of old men, ever ready with a word of advice to the 'young 'uns.' What has happened to the noble art of workmen watching? Are we all too busy to stop nowadays, or is it because we can't get near the men for machines?

The internal combustion engine and Oxford have had a long association and this old shot of the High Street, or The High, shows that traffic congestion is not entirely a modern phenomenon. The appearance of the vehicles suggests the inter-war years as all manner of traffic jostles for position. On the other hand, the names of Kodak and Mac Fisheries have a fairly modern ring about them, whilst Macs were to be found at Zac's for many years to come. The link between Oxford and motor-cars can be narrowed down to this very street, for it was at 48 High Street that

William Morris established his cycle shop in 1901. Fifty years ahead lay the British Motor Corporation at Cowley, with some 25,000 employees. Going the other direction in time, High Street was so called from the 1200s and it carried travellers towards the East Gate and London. With the rise of the coaching age in the 18th century, ancient inns in High Street, such as the Angel and Greyhound, became busy places. After a hard day in the traces, horses stabled at these inns would be turned loose to graze in the meadow visible from Magdalen Bridge.

Some interesting vehicles have been captured in this 'bird's eye' view from the top of Carfax Tower. The British Road Services wagon was a product of the nationalisation of road haulage in 1948 and this, along with dress of the pedestrians, suggests a date around 1950. The road surface at the top end of Cornmarket Street, an experimental creation of rubber blocks, is clearly visible, but would be gone by 1955. Precisely 600 years before this, in 1355, the view from Carfax Tower might well have been one of a mass of struggling men, as the perpetual rivalry and hatred between the students and citizens reached its peak in the Massacre of St Scholastica's Day, during which 63 students were killed. St Martin's Church had stood at the Carfax crossroads since 1032, although the tower was not built until the 14th century. Much of the rich history of Oxford has been enacted in its shadow. Beneath was once the 'Pennyless Bench,' for beggars. A great event was the building of the massive Carfax Conduit in 1616, which brought in piped water from Hinksey. It is said that it ran with beer or wine on celebratory occasions. Having been rebuilt in 1820/21, St Martin's was demolished in 1896, leaving only Carfax Tower and the historical perspectives it offers.

Below: It has to be admitted that the old Great Western Railway station off Botley Road (the site of the existing station) wasn't much to look at, but most railway travellers are less concerned with architectural magnificence than with trains running to time. In some ways it is the environs of the station that holds the interest in this 1940s shot - not just the line of vintage motors, but also the advertisement hoardings. There is a good deal of concern about 'inner cleanliness,' what with Andrews Liver Salts and Bile Beans. And as for dental hygiene, 'Did you Maclean your teeth today?' is one of the classics. Speed and convenience rather than the scope for advertising were probably the arguments put forward when the first Oxford railway was proposed in 1837. Nevertheless, powerful opposing interests managed to delay the opening of the GWR line until 1844. A second line opened in 1851, this time belonging to the London and North Western Railway, with its terminus at Rewley Road. Precisely 100 years later, in 1951, this station was closed. Meanwhile the GWR station had been rebuilt next door to Rewley Road, in 1852. It has remained on this site to the present day, with major alterations in 1910, 1970 and 1990.

Bottom: Clearly this is an important occasion for the employees of the City of Oxford Motor Services as they pose outside Cowley Road Garage in 1935. It is very much a matter of 'Sunday best,' or uniform, and well-polished shoes. The presence of medals and a vicar, however, suggests that it might be some solemn event relating to Remembrance Day. In contrast, the history of public road transport in Oxford had, at times, almost an element of farce about it. Although horse-drawn trams and buses had run successfully from the 1880s, so much controversy was aroused by the proposal to introduce electric tramcars that the Oxford Electric Tramway Company, formed in 1907, had spent £230,000 by 1913, with not a single tramcar running. By this time the Oxford ratepayers wanted motor buses, and William Morris (of automobile fame) forced the pace by running his own unlicensed buses from November 1913. He then happily moved aside to allow the Electric Tramway Company to take up the running of bus services from 1914 to 1921, when it became the City of Oxford Motor Services. Passengers grew in numbers until the 1950s, when competition from the private car forced the bus company to look for economies, and one-person operated buses were introduced in 1966.

Cycling and Oxford have always gone hand-in-hand, a vital link between people and their jobs

Jim Scaife, a spare part at the ready, stands at the door of his little shop at 83 London Road, Headington, in 1936. This was not yet the age of the car for most people, and having your own transport meant a bicycle for the vast majority. A few adventurous souls had motor-cycles, of course, and it looks like a rather nice Royal Enfield on display, with a well sprung saddle. Cycling and Oxford go hand-in-hand, even today, but in the 1930s it was a vital mode of transport linking people and their jobs. There were many little shops like Jim Scaife's dotted around, where you enjoy some personal attention, and in many instances talk to a fellow enthusiast. Quite often he would be able to nip out and make a quick diagnosis of your bicycle's problem, and possibly give it a quick fix on the spot. Garages tend to be on a bigger scale today, and lacking in that personal touch for car owners. There are some fine old cycle names on view outside Jim's shop, and the names of Meccano and Hornby might also cause a few eyes to glaze over with nostalgia. Model rail enthusiasts, of course, might have retained an unbroken link with Hornby - and their boyhoods.

Oxford's first speed trap snared 508 offenders in the first five months

Most of us have an ambivalent attitude towards the police, indignantly demanding a greater police presence when cars are stolen or vandalised, but fervently condemning all patrol cars and speed cameras to perdition if we are in a hurry and want to break the speed limit. What an outcry there was concerning the infringement of liberties when the breathalyser was introduced in the 1960s, and to a lesser extent when it was made compulsory to wear seat belts, and yet these measures have saved countless lives. The photograph shows members of the Oxfordshire Constabulary testing a speed trap in 1959.

It is uncertain as to whether the British Oxygen wagon just happens to be passing through, or whether it is standing by to revive trapped motorists with a quick whiff! The Traffic Department of Oxford City Police began to use PETA (Portable Electronic Traffic Analyser) in 1961. In spite of much press publicity, and large warning signs on roads, PETA snared 508 offenders in the first five months. The battle to drive home the message that 'Speed Kills' is a constant one, and the latest approach in urban areas has been 'traffic calming' - forcing motorists to reduce speed by inserting humps and creating obstacles, thus turning some roads into slalom courses.

Shopping spree

The Meat Market sign to the right indicates the destination of the contents of this fine old wagon in a High Street shot that dates back to the 1930s. The vehicle behind is sturdy enough to allow the young assistant to take a breather by sitting on the bumper - something you wouldn't be inclined to risk with most modern-day cars. But then things were built to last in those days, so much so that after 1945 to speak of something as being made 'pre-war' was to suggest quality and durability. The latter might well be the theme of the whole picture, for the late 18th century facade of the buildings on view still

exists today, as does the covered market concealed behind. Then again, 200 years or so is as nothing compared to the 1000 years timespan which has seen the centre of Oxford as host to a market. Evidence suggests around 900 AD for the appearance of the first market. By 1032 St Martin's, or Carfax Church, stood at the cross-roads in the centre of town, and the market naturally found its centre of gravity there. However, it soon spread down the High Street and was being held twice weekly by 1279. The covered market was completed in 1774, with 19th century extensions and re-roofings.

Think of 1930s department stores in Oxford and think of Webbers. There's no getting away from the name as it repeats itself in a variety of ways along its 18th century frontage. Even a modern chain store might think that this was a case of advertising 'overkill,' but what Charles Webber had purchased in 1905 had been not so much a store as a row of shops, numbers 9 to 15 High Street to be precise. Hence the need, or so he felt, to display the name of Webbers repeatedly to show that this was indeed a single enterprise. The frontage had been designed by John Gwynn as part of a grand entry to the covered

market to the rear. This opened in 1774, and indeed three pedestrian ways ran through Webbers to give access to it. Webbers claimed to have pioneered the use of telephones and electric lifts in department stores. This famous family firm was bought out in 1952, and closed down in 1971. More 18th century architecture, albeit of a more lofty kind, dominates the right-hand side of the picture. All Saints' Church built in 1708, became the city church from 1896, after the demolition of St Martin's at Carfax. Since 1975, however, it has served as the library for Lincoln College.

Businesses come and go, responding to shifting market trends, but it is always rather sad to see the 'Closing Down' sign. It seems to represent a business investment gone sour and high hopes dashed. Perhaps things went very well for a number of years until a whim of fashion turned the tide, resulting in declining trade and rising anxiety. Margetts, in Cornmarket Street, was still doing business in 1950. In spite of offering a range of other items - shirts, stockings, neckwear - the staple of its business had always been hats. The title of 'Hatter' is liberally sprinkled about, including an invitation to buy the 'Celebrated Lincoln Bennett Hats,'

which can be seen just above the door. Perhaps that was the problem. The wearing of hats passed out of fashion for the younger generation growing up after World War Two, whereas pre-war street scenes invariably show women in all variety of hats, and men often wearing flat caps, trilbies or homburgs. Both hat wearers and non-hat wearers are shown outside Margetts in a picture which dates from about 1950, and so probably the adverse trend had already begun. On the positive side, the cluster around the window shows that there were bargains to be had, and no doubt some new optimistic entrepreneur was waiting in the wings.

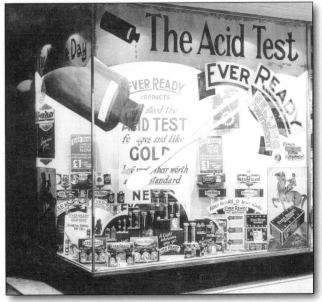

Top: Window dressing was taken to a fine art during the frequent window display competitions of the 1930s, and it must have taken much skill and care to assemble this one at Currys in Queen Street, which had branches at Cowley Road and St Ebbe's Street. The Union Jacks suggest a royal event, perhaps the Silver Jubilee of 1935 or the Coronation of 1937, but they may have been there simply to add a dash of patriotism to the advertised 'Sale.' The specialisms of Currys, cycles and wireless, represented an established leisure pursuit and a communications medium that was 'on the up.' Cycling has always been popular in and around Oxford, and not just among undergraduates. For many it has provided the ideal way to get to work, but as a leisure pursuit cycling became an absolute craze towards the end of the nineteenth century. William Morris had become the cycling champion of three counties by the time he set up his cycle repair business in East Oxford in 1893. The celebrated Morris Cycle, as sold on High Street by 1901, was a prelude to greater things. One of the most famous machines of later years, the Raleigh Cycle, could be bought in 1935 for £4 19s 6d, brand new with Sturmey-Archer three speed gears.

Left: A different Currys window display of the 1930s features another theme, this time the long-established brand of batteries, Ever Ready. The versatile battery could be used for torches and cycle lamps, but also for the wireless. 'Here's Health to your Radio' is proclaimed towards the bottom of the window. The radio, or wireless as it was then better known, assumed growing importance as a source of news and entertainment as more and more households acquired one between the wars. Little did Marconi know, as he sent his first signals over a distance of 1½ miles in Italy in 1894, that he was setting off a communications revolution. What really captured the public's imagination was when, in 1899, Marconi equipped two ships to report by wireless to New York on the progress of the Americas Cup yacht race. The medium never looked back, and many people shared in some of the defining moments of history by means of the radio - the abdication speech of Edward VIII in 1936; the sombre announcement by Neville Chamberlain, on September 3rd 1939, that Britain was at war with Germany. What a long way we have come from twiddling the knobs on the dial, and speculating about strange names such as Hilversum, to transistors and printed circuits.

Queen Street, one of the four principal streets which meet at the Carfax crossroads, once took travellers to and from the old western gate. Known as the Great Bailey in the 13th century, and later Butcher Row, it took on its present name after the visit to Oxford of George III, and his wife Queen Charlotte, in 1785. If that speaks of change, well then constant change is part of the organic development of towns and cities. This view of the south side of Queen Street was right up-to-date in the 1950s, including the Morris Minor. Badcocks was a fashion store of long-standing. Back in the 1930s it was offering 'Swagger Coats' at prices ranging from 29/11d (£1.50) to 63s (£3.15). Ladies' figures could be 'moulded to beauty' by Berlei foundation garments. To the right of Badcocks stood the Electra Cinema, originally opened in March 1911, featuring pictures of the boat race as its first day attraction. By the 1950s, as the poster outside proclaims, Robert Donat was one of the stars of the day. The prospect is now completely different. The Electra closed in 1958, making way for a Co-operative store. This in turn disappeared, along with the Badcocks building, to create a new Marks & Spencer store in 1978.

At work

If ever a brand of marmalade has been a household name - particularly in the 'best' houses - it must surely have been Frank Cooper's 'Oxford' Marmalade. In Nancy Mitford's novel spanning the 1920s and 1930s, 'The Pursuit of Love,' when Uncle Matthew at the breakfast table says, 'Cooper's, Oxford, please,' everyone instantly knows what he is referring to, and that there can be no substitute. The two photographs show the firm apparently in busy mode in September 1942. The virtually all-female packing department *(below)* is handling a large quantity of tins. Clearly this is meant to be a standing-up job, although one girl has found herself a makeshift chair in the shape of a rather uncomfortable looking packing case. The second photograph *(right)* moves the process a stage or two further, to the despatch department, where boxes of marmalade stand ready to go. However, these may well have been the last boxes for several years, for in October 1942 it was announced that Frank Cooper's factory had been requisitioned by the government for wartime purposes, and that the manufacture of 'Oxford' Marmalade must stop until after the war. The founder of its marmalade empire, Frank

Cooper, was born over his father's shop at 46 High Street, in 1844. Groceries and tea were his family's stock in trade, but Frank entered the much more profitable field of marmalade in 1874. Tradition has it that it was Frank's go-ahead wife, Sarah Jane, who produced the first batch of 182 lbs the same year. This was done in the kitchens of the old Angel Hotel, so adjacent to the Examination Schools that the poor students must have suffered mightily if the mouth-watering scents of boiling marmalade drifted up to them whilst they were, perhaps, 'wrestling with Plato.' Business boomed, and by 1903 the Cooper enterprise had moved to a purpose-built factory at Park End Street, close to railway links. In 1914 a small family company was formed to run the business, and it remained in family hands until it was taken over by the food company, CPC, in 1964. At this point production was transferred away from Oxford. Cooper's marmalade, with its distinctive taste and high quality, seemed to belong to that leisurely aristocratic world of the inter-war years - to country houses, officers' messes and London clubs. It figured largely in the life of Oxford undergraduates too, who fondly termed it 'squish.'

Elliston & Cavell was the largest department store in Oxford in the 1930s

The Packing Room at Elliston and Cavell Ltd in the 1930s offers a fascinating glimpse into the female hairstyles of the day, and no doubt a few of them were modelled on the current heroines of the silver screen. There is a good deal of brown paper, sticky tape and string in evidence, and judging by the quantity of parcels stacked around the room, the firm was doing good business. The work was perhaps a little tedious, but it gave employment to a good number, and as Elliston and Cavell was the largest department store in Oxford at this time, the numbers in this room would have been multiplied many times over. The business began with the setting up of a draper's shop in Magdalen Street, in 1823, by Jesse Elliston. By 1835 he and James Cavell had entered into a partnership which prospered. Expansion involved the amalgamation and adaptation of adjoining property, resulting in an interesting variety of architectural styles. Among the great range of goods being offered by Elliston and Cavell in 1935, 100 years after the partnership had been formed, were deck chairs at 3/9d (17½p) and garden couch hammocks at just short of £4. In 1953 the store was taken over by Debenham's, although the old name was retained until 1973.

The automatic telephone exchange at Pembroke Street served Oxford between 1926 and 1959, and the photograph shows a busy scene at the auto-manual board in 1947. The image of the telephone from that time is of something that only belonged to well-to-do folk. It was always black, rested on a cradle, and when ringing up

there were usually only four numbers or less to remember. The volume of subscribers in 1945 seems to confirm that the telephone was very much a luxury item. Oxford Central numbered only 3930, whilst Summertown had 1789 and Headington 1057. However, by 1949 there was a waiting list of 6314, and the steady

rise in telephone ownership was underway. Pembroke Street soon began to feel the pressure, and in 1954 a relief manual room had to be opened with 19 extra positions. Nevertheless conditions were cramped and it was a great relief when a new automatic exchange was opened at Speedwell Street in 1959. The first call out of the new exchange was made by the Postmaster-General, Ernest Marples, who also inaugurated Oxford's Speaking Clock service. The pace of change since then has accelerated enormously, and the switchboard girls of 1947 could never have anticipated the world of answering machines, e-mails and mobile phones.

Coal was the main driving force behind the building of the Oxford Canal

No, these are not 1930s heroines of the Soviet Union, on course for completing one of Stalin's Five Year Plans in record time. They are strong and determined looking women of Oxford, unloading coal from a barge at a canal wharf in August 1956. Coal was the main driving force behind the building of the Oxford Canal, running from Hawkesbury (near Coventry) to New Road, Oxford. It was neither an easy nor a cheap venture, for the 91 mile stretch cost £307,000, and took from 1769 to 1790 to make. The benefit, however, lay in the fact that it gave Oxford direct access to Midlands coal. This could be brought more quickly and cheaply to Oxford than coal which previously had been shipped from the North-East to London, then transferred to barges to come up the Thames. The Duke of Marlborough built a cut at Wolvercote, linking the canal to the Thames. He owned Wolvercote Paper Mill, and between 1811 and 1952 100 tons of coal per week came through Duke's Cut to feed the steam engine at the mill. As with most canals, railway competition proved too much, and by 1955 virtually all commercial traffic had ceased on the Oxford Canal. The 1968 Transport Act rescheduled it as 'a recreation and amenity waterway.'

Above: Industrial empires rise and fall, and this great sprawl of workshops and railway sidings in 1939 marked the Cowley empire of William Morris, entrepreneur of genius. From running a little cycle repair business In East Oxford in 1893, he superintended the growth of a business empire which, at its peak in 1973, was employing 28,500 people. Vision and the willingness to back his own judgement marked out his career, and he was quick to perceive that the future lay with the motor car. His immediate aim was to produce his own, and with an advance order for 400, he utilised the old Military College at Cowley, turning out the first production model of the 'Morris-Oxford Light Car,' with its distinctive 'bullnose' radiator, in March 1913. At the end of 1914 he had sold 1,300 cars. By the mid-1920s, using price cutting as a weapon against the post-war slump, Morris was selling cars by the thousand. The millionth Morris car rolled off the assembly line in 1939, and the two millionth in 1952, but of all models perhaps the Minor and the Mini have left the greatest mark. William Morris was made Lord Nuffield in 1938. He died in 1963, having given away £30 million of his fortune, but only a small fragment of his old empire now remains at Cowley.

Right: The 1960s were years of expansion for many firms and the Pressed Steel Company at Cowley was no exception. This picture of the huge crane and new office block under construction in 1961 seems to symbolise a growth era that was to continue into the 1970s. The company began its life as an offshoot of Morris Motors when, in 1926, William Morris joined with the Budd Manufacturing Company of Philadelphia, and the merchant bankers Schroeder, to form the Pressed Steel Company. Adjoining the Morris factory at Cowley, Pressed Steel's contribution to the mass-production process was in the use of huge power-presses to stamp out car body panels. The latter were then welded together into complete car bodies. The company became independent in 1930, which allowed it to build bodies for other car manufacturers. However, Morris Motors remained a major customer, and Pressed Steel shared in the rapid growth of that company. Growth can be rather an abstract concept, and to put it in more graphic terms, the first press shop at Cowley was longer than the Houses of Parliament, and an additional one built in 1938 was almost as long as St Paul's Cathedral. Similarly, the Pressed Steel Company employed 546 people in 1926, and over 9,000 by 1960.
Continued overleaf

Any company this size becomes almost a community, and in some respects begins to take on the characteristics of one. In so doing, community spirit can be translated into company spirit. Pensions, life insurance schemes, canteens and recreational clubs are quite normal in this respect, but Pressed Steel was large enough to have its own hospital *(below)*, with two resident doctors, a dentist and a physiotherapist, along with numerous first aid posts. The photograph, from the 1950s, shows a nurse who gives an impression of brisk efficiency, whilst a casualty sits on the treatment bed. The figure in the other bed looks very young, and

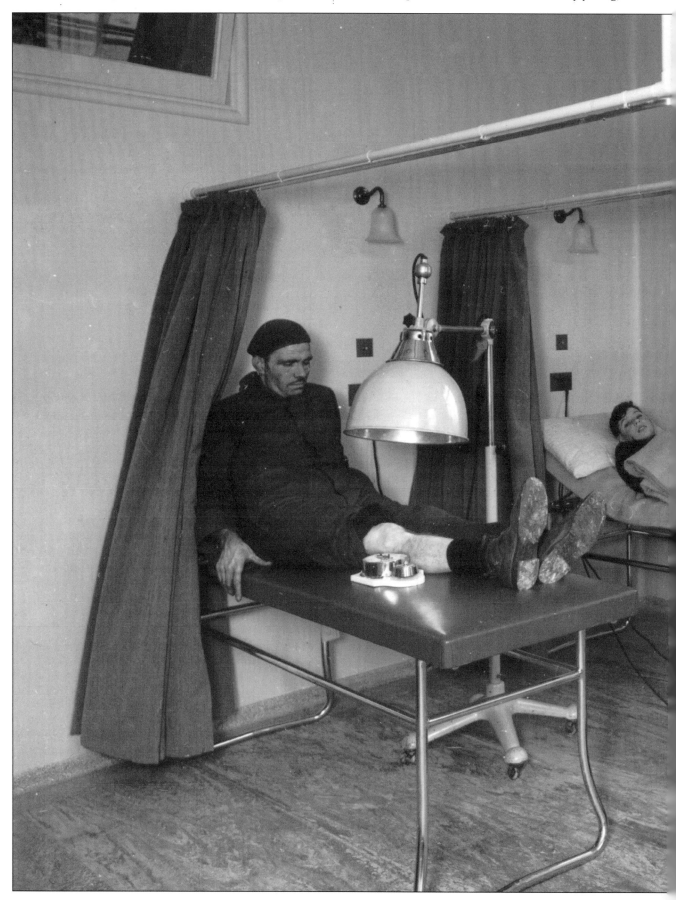

possibly he was an apprentice. One very unusual feature of the Pressed Steel Company had to do more with practicality than welfare. It had its own fire brigade so that it was self-reliant in case of emergencies, and two of the firemen and equipment are pictured overleaf in 1958. The fire-fighting team must have been an efficient one, for it won numerous cups in competitions. This readiness and good training may have been a legacy of the second world war, when the company had a permanently manned Air Raid Precaution control room, area wardens and 400 volunteers, partly with fire-fighting in mind.

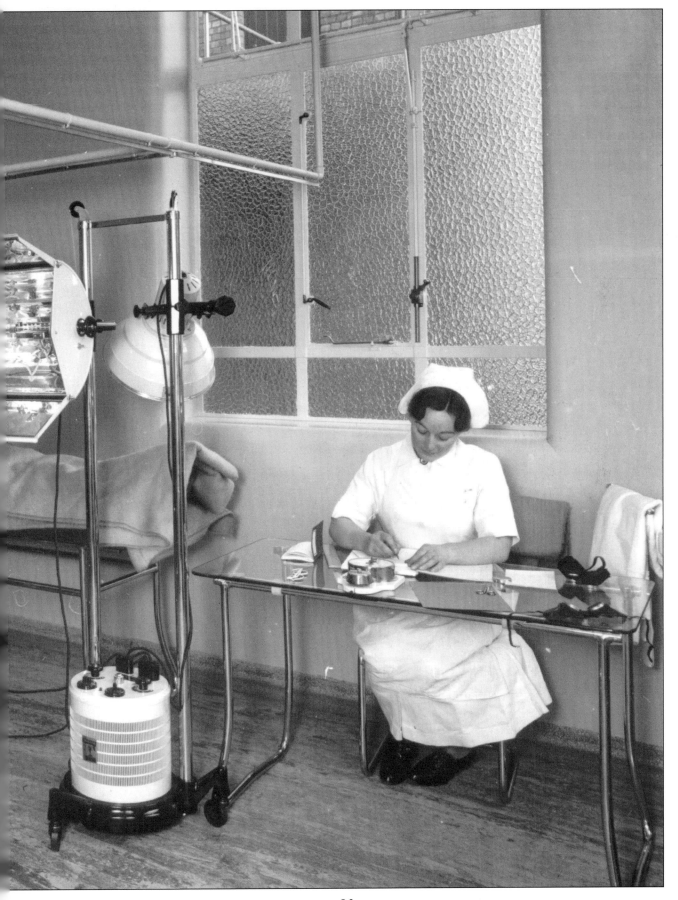

During the war, Pressed Steel produced over 23,000 tons of steel and 27,000 tons of light alloy

The efforts of the Pressed Steel workers during the war were impressive. Both men and women laboured long hours on war work. Pressed Steel alone produced over 23,000 tons of steel and 27,000 tons of light alloy, and in combination with the Nuffield factories the company churned out a steady stream of planes, tanks, torpedoes, wirelesses, searchlights, machine gun tripods, sea mines and depth charges. The post-war years saw Pressed Steel return to making car bodies, but enjoying success elsewhere in the shape of Prestcold refrigerators. First produced in 1932, and using techniques that proved useful during the war in some respects, this side of the company's output boomed after the war. It was not simply a matter of domestic refrigerators. Prestcold equipment was used to create coldstores on ships, to refrigerate food on aeroplanes, to keep beer cellars cool and even to store Lincolnshire tulip bulbs. Closer to home, through Prestcold the Wingfield Morris Hospital was able to preserve portions of bone for future bone-grafting operations, whilst at Morris Motors engines could be tested under Arctic conditions. In 1965 Pressed Steel joined the combined Morris-Austin company, the British Motor Corporation, to form British Motor Holdings, thus ending up where it had started out in 1926.

Engineering brilliant solutions with quality and service

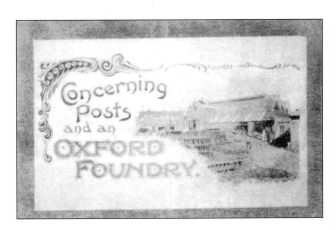

It is believed that the origins of W Lucy & Co Ltd, reach as far back as 1760. Indeed, a pre-1914 catalogue supports this belief in its claim that the company was established in this year. The accuracy of this date can be debated. However, as existing records prove, the company has certainly been in existence since 1812. It was in this year that William Carter opened a shop in Oxford High Street trading as, 'an ironmonger, hardware, brazier and tinplate worker'.

By 1821 William now calling himself a general manufacturer had made such a success of his business that he started manufacturing his own goods. His business continued to grow and after moving to a new brass and iron foundry at Summertown he moved again in 1825 to the site which the company still occupies today. This site known then as the Jericho Iron and Brass Foundry was advantageously located next to the Oxford to Birmingham Canal indeed some of the initial agricultural machinery and ornamental ironwork produced from this site was still being made a century later!

In 1827 William's manufacturing company had become so successful that he was able to concentrate solely on that side of the business and thus, could sell his shop. Always moving forward, three years later, William left his company to his partners, Grafton, Baker, and Biggs in order to continue as an ironmonger in Leamington.

Grafton seems to have been the governor of the business, with various changes in partners until his death in 1861. It was he, in 1838, that changed the name of the business to 'Eagle'

*Top: A Lucy publication dated 1902 advertising cast-iron lamp posts. **Top right:** J R Dick, who became Managing Director of the company in 1905. **Right:** Pillar Assembly at the Walton Meadow site in the late 1950s.*

ironworks and developed its links with the building industry. Many of its products such as the 'Lucy lamp posts' can still be found today.

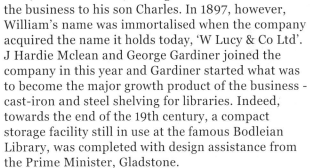

In 1864, a young William Lucy took over the business. Sadly, William died of tuberculosis in 1873 aged just 35, leaving James Kelley free to buy the business. Only six years later, James too died, leaving the business to his son Charles. In 1897, however, William's name was immortalised when the company acquired the name it holds today, 'W Lucy & Co Ltd'. J Hardie Mclean and George Gardiner joined the company in this year and Gardiner started what was to become the major growth product of the business - cast-iron and steel shelving for libraries. Indeed, towards the end of the 19th century, a compact storage facility still in use at the famous Bodleian Library, was completed with design assistance from the Prime Minister, Gladstone.

The company experienced financial and production difficulties during the early 1900s but with the arrival of William Leonard Madgen and his electrical engineering expertise, the business began to recover. Madgen hired John Reid Dick as the manager for the company. J R Dick is remembered as a neat, brisk, shrewd but kind man who always wore a fresh rose in his buttonhole but, more importantly as the man who helped to secure 'Lucy's' long-term future. The company was the first to develop and manufacture the above-ground feeder pillar and in the years

before the first world war the company enjoyed orders from Belfast to Bombay. Despite securing a long-term future, by 1907 the business was still not financially secure. The short story writer and poet, A E Coppard, who worked for the company as a confidential clerk and book keeper, later described 'Lucy's' finances at the time as, 'lower than low water'!

The advent of the first world war brought with it extensive changes for 'Lucy's'. The company used its foundry and engineering equipment to produce munitions, concentrating on the production of mine sinkers and mortar bombs. During the inter-war years, with advances in the electricity market, the company had to face the fact that that its future was in switchgear and electrical engineering. The outbreak of the second world war saw 'Lucy's' mainly dependent on its foundry for components. The lack of equipment meant that by 1940, profits had fallen to an all-time low. With the threat of closure, the company was forced to improvise and as a result made a simple lathe which was used in shell production. This enabled the company to remain afloat and indeed become very busy throughout the rest of the war.

After the war years the company embarked upon an intensive programme of modernisation and increased self-sufficiency introducing bakelite components and plastics. A generating plant was installed to cope with the frequent power cuts experienced after the war. This generator remained

Top: *Castle Mill, taken in the late 1980s.*
Above centre: *A Soag-Oxford Heavy-duty Purpose Lathe, designed and manufactured during World War II.* **Right:** *The factory entrance at night.*

the only source of power up until 1984 when a switch was made to the public electricity supply. In 1960, a short-circuit station was also installed to enable full in-house testing of equipment.

The 1960s were marked by a change in the industrial scene and consequently another dip in sales for the company. In 1969 annual sales fell from £2.7 million to £1.8 million, profit was almost nil and the number of employees were reduced from 855 to 609. Once again survival rested on the innovation of the company. Gordon Dick became Chairman in 1951 on the death of his father and appointed Ralph Holland who later became a Director of the company. It was Ralph who provided this innovation by moving the factory to its present structure of three distinct trading entities and developing a wide range of overseas markets.

This innovative approach led to a dramatic change in fortunes for the company. The two decades from 1970 to 1990 saw 'Lucy's' grow into an international company. A new range of oil-filled high voltage ring main units was developed making 'Lucy's' the biggest manufacturer of this equipment in the world.

This success was achieved in several ways. It began when the 'Teheran Electric Company' put in a major order for feeder pillars. Despite a delay in the process, when Ralph Holland was prevented from signing the contract in Teheran as his papers were rejected as insufficient evidence of his identity, the contract was finally completed in the more mundane surroundings of his office in

achieved in 1996 with the construction of a new plant at Thame for the production of volume castings. Around the same time investment was made in another facility at Witney for larger low volume castings; this has allowed the production to continue of some of Lucy's traditional products -including the cast iron pillar and street lamp brackets, many of which were installed in St Giles and surrounding roads during the late 90s.

A feature of the switchgear business in the 1990s has been the establishment of companies outside the U.K. in Saudi Arabia, India and South Africa. This has helped to maintain the high level of overseas sales in the very competitive market conditions.

Lucy's may have originally entered the property business unintentionally, but today the development, management, and letting of its property portfolio are a major part of the Company's operations. The success of this activity has certainly been assisted by the continuing popularity of Oxford as an international centre of learning and by the growth of knowledge-based businesses in the area.

The next decade will certainly require further significant changes within Lucy's and all those who work within this long established Company are ready for the challenges this will produce.

Top left: A Rotary Transfer machine, 1990.
Above: An aerial view of the factory in 1988.
Below: Lucy Castings, Thame 1997.

1972. This marked a growth in the export to overseas markets. Indeed, the largest ever order received came in 1980 from Riyadh and was worth £2.4 million and in 1986 'The Saudi Lucy Company Limited' was founded. Substantial developments to the actual workings of the business were also made during these years including, the installation of numerous new and more efficient pieces of equipment and systems, and the building of 34 more flats and a new warehouse known as the 'Palace'!

The 3rd September 1990 marked the end of an era for Lucy with the death of Gordon Dick after 60 years' service. He was succeeded as Chairman by his youngest son, Richard, the third generation of the family to be involved with the Company.

The early part of the decade brought recession, the Gulf War, and the privatisation of the electricity utilities in Britain - some of Lucy's most important customers. To meet these changing conditions the firm has focused its activities into three core areas - the traditional ones of manufacturing castings and switchgear but also into property.

The relocation of its castings business from Oxford had been an objective for the Company from as far back as 1938 when a site to the north of the city was acquired This was finally

A very fruitful family business

As the 20th century got underway, the regular customers who went to Mr and Mrs Hicks' shop in Stanley Road, Oxford for their fruit and vegetables would have no doubt taken a great interest in the succession of new arrivals into the Hicks family. The Hicks had eight children, five boys and three girls, and it was not long before some of the youngsters began to show their faces in the shop and make themselves useful in the family business. The second eldest, Harold, born in 1902, particularly enjoyed helping, and spent many a happy hour working for his parents after school and in the holidays. He also had a great love of horses; he was a spirited lad, and caused his parents great consternation when, in spite of being too young, he resolved to join up on the outbreak of war. Eventually his father managed to talk him out of faking his age, and Harold stayed at home and carried on working with his parents.

In addition to the shop, the family had another building where they stored produce, which they always referred to as their warehouse, and it was this side of the business which attracted young Harold. He liked going out buying; in those days it was not uncommon to purchase an orchard and pick the produce, and this was one of the things that Harold used to do. Sourcing and selecting produce was, to Harold, much more interesting than serving in the shop.

Harold became engaged to a young lady named Mary Winifred, who taught at the infants school, and the couple were married on Empire Day, 1926. Mary gave up teaching and threw herself wholeheartedly into the family business; Harold bought two cottages in Magdalen Road and turned the lower half into a shop, where the young couple started a business of their own. This soon became a very profitable enterprise. Harold began wholesaling from the rear of the shop, and trade soon built up. When the wholesaling side needed more

Above left: *Harold Hicks, founder of the company.*
Below: *The original shop at No 72 Magdalen Street.*

space than the shop could offer, additional premises were acquired a short distance away. A little further along were Harold's banana ripening rooms.

During the 20s the horses and carts of his father's day had begun to make way for motor transport, and Harold built up a motorised fleet, acquiring now-classic vehicles like Model T Fords, Commers and Fordsons and using Scammel 3-wheelers, affectionately known as iron horses, for short haul. The arrival of motor transport made it possible to collect produce from a wider area. Harold started going to Covent Garden market during the late 1920s, and by the time the second world war broke out he was also sourcing produce from Lincolnshire, Cambridgeshire and Bedfordshire, and also via Southampton and Sharpness Docks in Liverpool.

Harold had fulfilled his early ambitions to establish himself in the fruit and vegetable trade in a remarkably short time; however, another of his childhood dreams was destined never to come true. Having been too young to join up in the first world war, he found that his country had other plans for him in the second world war too: he was to service the many military bases, both air force and army, over an area extending as far south as Portsmouth.

The war years were a worrying time for Harold not only because of trading complexities but also because of the ill-health of his older brother which left him too weak to conduct his own business. With Jack's two sons away on active service, Harold took upon himself the responsibility of keeping his brother's affairs afloat. In 1943 he merged the two ventures to run them as a single concern; and only six months after these arrangements had been made, Jack died.

Jack's sons returned in 1945. By this time, too, Harold's son had been born, giving him a fresh incentive to build up the family business. He was impatient to expand, and as soon as the wartime building restrictions were lifted the company had new banana ripening rooms built,

Above left: *One of the earliest company vehicles.*
Top: *The 1950s fleet.*

which were considered to be the finest anywhere in the country. Trade began to flourish again. The business association between uncle and nephews continued for twelve years, but by 1955 Harold felt that he had done all he could to help the young men, and decided to separate off his own interests. A 3/4 acre orchard site became available - situated, by remarkable co-incidence, in Percy Street, just round the corner from Magdelan Road where he had first started out in business almost 30 years earlier - which Harold bought and developed into a wholesale distribution warehouse.

In due course he was joined by his three sons. The business grew, operating over a 20 to 30 mile radius of Oxford - from Witney and Burford in the north to Newbury and Reading in the south, and from Aylesbury in the east to Swindon in the west. Harold was employing a staff of around ten besides the family; one of his employees at this time was 'Pud' Puddifer, who had begun working for the Hicks family while they still had their shop in Magdelan Road. Pud had transferred over to the wholesale side when the shop was sold, had been called up during the war, and had then rejoined the firm when he was demobbed. He was to continue

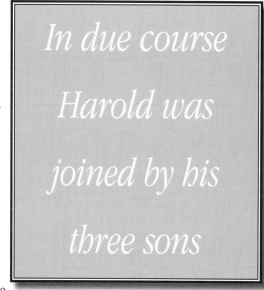

In due course Harold was joined by his three sons

working for Hicks until 1996, the last few years on a part-time basis, and earned the distinction of being the company's longest-serving employee.

Harold Hicks died in 1992, of a broken heart, after losing his wife just six months previously. His death was a great blow not only to his family but to all those who had had dealings with him. He was held in the greatest esteem in the trade, and had in fact been chosen to represent the country's provincial wholesalers in the controversy surrounding the closure of the old Covent Garden site and transfer of the market to Nine Elms.

The business was left to Harold's three sons. Sadly, the eldest, Basil, died only a year later. The youngest was less interested in the business, and so it was the middle brother, Malcolm, who eventually took over the running of the firm after this tragic and difficult period, made the worse when a close personal friend who also worked in the business suffered a bereavement at around the same time.

Above: *The fleet from the 1960s outside the firm's premises.*

Malcolm Hicks had begun working at Percy Street straight after finishing college in 1957. As in many a family firm, the youngsters started at the bottom, working in the warehouse, driving the van, and getting a thorough grounding in all aspects of the business before being allowed to take on more responsibility. Later on Malcolm, along with his brothers, progressed into selling, buying and the operation of the transport fleet. During this period changes in the nation's lifestyle had a considerable effect on the wholesale fruit and vegetable trade. Cheaper air travel meant more people holidaying in exotic places where they developed a liking for previously unheard-of vegetables such as peppers and aubergines; so the range of produce available in this country grew much wider to cater for changing tastes. Also, fruit and vegetables which had previously been seasonal were now displayed in the shops all year round,

either frozen, or flown in fresh from the other side of the world. And freezers, coupled with the coming of the supermarket, changed the pattern of shopping for ever, bringing about the demise of many corner shops in the process. Daily shopping became a thing of the past, replaced by a weekly or even a monthly shopping expedition to stock up on frozen produce. All these changes took place in the latter half of the 20th century, so that the wholesale business which Malcolm took over in the 1990s was pretty different from the one where he had started work almost half a century earlier.

In 1995 the company moved to its current premises in Pony Road, Oxford, which are easily reached via the ring road and are better suited generally to the needs of the present day. Hicks is not a company which seeks change for its own sake. It is a business built on experience and

a thorough understanding of the wholesale trade. But it is also a business which has evolved with the times, exploring new opportunities and adapting to shifts in the trading pattern. These sound principles have enabled the family firm not only to survive but to thrive for a period of 75 years, handed down from father to son. During this period many challenges have been faced and many difficulties overcome, and the consistently sound decisions and hard work of the Harold Hicks and his son Malcolm, assisted by their loyal staff, have brought well-deserved success. As Harold Hicks Limited approaches its 75th anniversary, it can look back on its history, thus far, with pride.

Left: *Harold Hicks in a banana plantation in the Canary Islands.*
Below: *The 1970s fleet.*

The cultivation of success

The Wood family were farmers in Lisemore, County Waterford, Southern Ireland. In 1927 the family were forced to move away. They left from Belfast and arrived in Liverpool. Because of the farming background the immigration department made land available at Ford Village nr Aylesbury, Buckinghamshire. There were four children and they all attended school in Aylesbury. Part of the daily routine was to milk the cows, then deliver the milk in churns to the Dairy in Aylesbury and then go to school.

John Wood spent any spare time working at home gaining experience that was to prove invaluable later on in his successful career. John had a burning desire to be able to fly. This was the main driving force in his life. Spurred on by his passion for flying, John was now ready and extremely eager to set up his own business as he realised that his long standing ambition was a costly one to fulfil. In order to become a pilot and be able to afford to fly, John had to devise a way to make money.

John Wood's money making venture started life before the advent of the second world war. His father assigned four acres of land at the family farm in Ford Village to him for a trial period to see if he could make a success of this unique opportunity. John tried anything that he thought would make him a profit. In these early days the four acres were used for several projects from growing blackcurrants to rearing turkeys. He also rented land for growing potatoes and corn. However, the decision to start to grow mushrooms on the four acre plot was to be the defining moment of what was to become the

Right: *John Wood about to board a plane in 1942 as a fighter pilot.*
Below: *Elmwood Farm, 1954.*

successful and prosperous Aylesbury Mushrooms Limited!

Soon after starting work on the four acre plot of land loaned to him by his father, rent free, John was able to purchase the site. At the same time he also bought three second hand sheds which were all insulated with hay placed between tongued and grooved panels. These sheds were bought, taken down, and moved for what would be the modern day equivalent of £35 each!

John Wood's entrepreneurial spirit had to be temporarily repressed with the advent of the second world war. During the war his business was shut down but his ambition was still active. By this time John had already taught himself how to fly and was impatient to put his skills to use by serving his country at war. Initially he was turned down by the Royal Air Force who wanted to enlist people who had no experience of flying so that they could be trained from scratch as RAF pilots. As the war progressed however, John's services were called upon. He served in the Royal Air Force as a bomber pilot, a fighter pilot, a test pilot and a ferry pilot, delivering bombers wherever they were needed and as an instructor training much needed pilots. Bombing missions took a considerable amount of bravery of the whole crew. More often than not, the crews would set off with the knowledge that out of twenty planes taking off on a mission, only two might return. On one of these missions his younger brother, Frank, did not return. One of his more unusual missions was to be involved in a compassionate flight to drop some artificial legs for Douglas Bader who was a prisoner of war in Germany.

It was as an instructor at Perth in Scotland that John Wood met Margaret Morton, who also served in the Royal Air Force. At the close of the war he and Margaret were married, they also added the Stewart to their name as they knew there were a lot of Woods in the Aylesbury area. It was then that the Stewart-Woods business was resumed. Indeed, in 1945 the business was officially registered and Aylesbury Mushrooms Limited was established. The couple set to work together and Margaret sold and delivered the mushrooms leaving her husband to make the compost and actually grow the mushrooms. The Stewart-Woods also employed Prisoners of war at this time to help to build up the business and indeed, many of them stayed on for years after the war. They were very loyal employees.

Above left: *John Stewart-Wood with an Auster he used to fly between the farm at Aylesbury and the farm at Elmwood.*
Top: *Preparation of mushroom compost.*

The history of the mushroom is itself an interesting one seeped in folklore. According to the Hieroglyphics of 4600 years ago Mr and Mrs Stewart-Wood were not the only ones to favour the mushroom. The ancient Egyptians believed that the mushroom was the plant of immortality and the flavour of mushrooms intrigued the pharaohs so much that they decreed that mushrooms were food for royalty and that no commoner could ever touch them. In other civilisations throughout the world including Russia, China, Greece, Mexico and Latin America, mushroom rituals were practiced. Many believed that mushrooms had properties that could produce super human strength, help in finding lost objects and lead the soul to the realm of the gods! The formal cultivation of mushrooms is thought to have begun in France and some accounts say that Louis XIV was the first mushroom grower culti-vating mushrooms in special caves near Paris!

If not discovering the fabled attributes of the mushroom, Mr and Mrs Stewart-Wood did at first have to cope with some of its other mysterious qualities. Learning how to grow the mushrooms in the most efficient and effective way was a learning curve for the couple. Mushrooms are a

unique growing vegetable and mushroom growing is an unusual process. To begin with the mushrooms are fungi and so grow from microscopic spores, not seeds. These spores have to be collected in almost sterile environments and used to inoculate grains or seeds to produce a product called spawn. Mushrooms are also grown in the dark because they have no chlorophyll and get all their nutrients from organic matter in their compost - which itself takes one to two weeks to prepare! Mr and Mrs J Stewart-Wood had to cope with the complicated processes

Below: *The main entrance to Aylesbury Mushrooms.*
Bottom: *An aerial view of the company.*

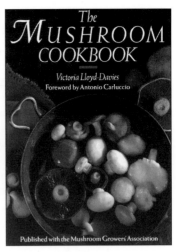

involved in cultivating mushrooms as well as dealing with the shortage of raw materials at the time. Therefore, due to these problems, they, along with other like minded mushroom growers decided to set up a group in which they could all share their ideas, successes and failures and in doing so learn from each other. This group was established in 1948 and was named, the Mushroom Growers' Association. The Association is still in operation today and is now based at Stamford, Lincolnshire.

By 1949 Aylesbury Mushrooms Limited was flourishing, so much so that the Stewart-Woods could afford to expand the business. When John Stewart-Wood viewed Elmwood farm with its many dairy buildings, he immediately saw the potential for converting these buildings into growing rooms for the mushrooms. Subsequently, John purchased Elmwood farm at Black Bourton and in doing so developed his business even further.

Margaret and John Stewart-Wood had three children, Vivienne, Jeannette and Frank. In 1967, over 20 years after Aylesbury Mushrooms Limited was established, Frank became the second Stewart-Wood generation to be involved in what could then be called, the family business. Before joining the business Frank had spent time on the farm helping his father out. In the years 1967 and 1968 however, Frank spent his time in Montreal and Toronto gaining experience on different mushroom farms there.

With Frank's help the business continued to thrive and in 1979 the Stewart-Woods decided to consolidate operations. The Ford farm, which had been used by the family since 1928, was sold along with the mushroom business that it contained. More buildings were built at Elmwood farm in compensation. The business was still running from Elmwood when it celebrated its 50th anniversary in 1995 and indeed, is currently based at Elmwood.

The company's six refrigerated lorries deliver the mushrooms to the wholesale retailers and pub

chains throughout the UK. In conjunction with the Mushroom Growers' Association, the Stewart-Woods advertise their produce mainly through women's magazines although, the Marching Mushrooms television advertising campaign was a memorable and successful sideline. Indeed, the Association have also produced the first hardback book on cooking with cultivated mushrooms published in Great Britain to advertise the flexibility of the vegetable.

As the Stewart-Wood family take Aylesbury Mushrooms Limited towards its centenary the business continues to thrive. The ambition and entrepreneurial spirit of its founder, John Stewart-Wood, is still in abundance as are the quality mushrooms which, with their wide appeal, continue to be as popular, if not as rare, as they were in Egyptian times!

Top left and below: Publicity pictures of mushrooms. *Top right:* The Mushroom Cookbook, published with the Mushroom Growers' Association.

High class service from a family firm...

WG Powell Ltd, Timber and Builders Merchants, of Cowley Road, Oxford is a company with a long tradition in supplying all things wood, but who have kept bang up to date with the requirements of their clients. From a beginning which saw Walter Powell, in 1923, building sheds, greenhouses and dog kennels in his back garden, the firm has advanced to the stage where they supply not only the doors, flooring, staircases and mouldings (machined to order) which might be expected, but also all items for the do-it yourself enthusiast. Double glazed units are made to order; glass cutting is done on a while-you-wait basis; and - possibly the most recent of the additions to supplies - garden decking can be provided to the specific requirements of the particular client. With decking being heavily promoted on all the television gardening programmes at the moment this must be a boon to all those following the latest exterior design trends. But, back to the beginning, in that back garden...

Whilst Walter Powell was busy selling his sheds, hen houses and assorted other wooden items from home, he began being asked for raw timber as well. As the timber had to be stocked in order to make the items for sale, it made sense to sell it if that was what clients required. A simple response to customer needs, but it was the start of the expansion of the company which hasn't stopped yet. Luckily the garden was a good size, but it did mean initially sacrificing the tennis courts! Gradually the whole area of the garden was taken over for storage - a problem which must have worsened with the huge increase in demand occasioned by the shortages of the war years. By then, however, Mr Powell had built his own best publicity in the form of a new Tudor style house for himself and his family at Iffley Road in Oxford. As the company was being rebuilt after the war, Mr Powell was re-joined by Tom Edgington, described as 'the practical man', who became ultimately a director of the firm, and between them they concentrated largely on the wide variety of high quality portable buildings for which they had made their name.

In 1964, Helen Pearson, Mr. Powell's daughter joined the company and in the same year Paul Quarterman started as an apprentice. In 1999 he was appointed a director, having been general manger for many years.

Below: *The company's first lorry in the 1920s.*
Bottom: *The staff and family in the 1950s just after the company's new lorry had been delivered.*

publicity for the business, but also ensure the company's boast of same-day or next-day delivery anywhere within the Oxford Ring Road, and next-day delivery to any of the other areas they serve, is met. Powells is still an independent company, one of only two independent timber merchants in the city. Their expertise is particularly beneficial within a university city boasting many old buildings requiring programmes of continuous maintenance.

It seems clear from their focus on the customer, their rapid response to their clients' needs, and their willingness to diversify when necessary, that this is a business with every intention of continuing Walter Powell's vision well into the future. He was not wrong when he said - well ahead of his time - that he could see no reason why a woman should not head a company like his. He would be proud of the way the business he started in his back garden is being nurtured by his daughters and their colleagues in whom he put his faith.

In 1982, Walter Powell died, leaving the family business in the hands of Helen Pearson, who is Managing Director to this day. Under her management, and that of her three sisters who are all also directors, the company has expanded and developed into the complete service for both proponents of do-it-yourself and trade customers. Not only timber is supplied, but ironmongery, glass, and anything else the client may need. The company prides itself on still being a family-run firm, and indeed, many of those members of staff who are not family have been with Powells so long (many since they left school) that they feel like family!

So how have W G Powell managed to not only survive but expand in these days of DIY superstores? The answer is clear - commitment to service to the customer. The development of the company has always been based on responding to customer needs. Not only that, a fleet of personalised delivery vehicles serve not only as mobile

Above left: *The premises at 474 Cowley Road.*
Top: *The timber store in the 1920s.*
Below: *Today's fleet.*

Nature well nurtured

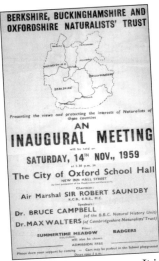

November 1999 marks the 40th anniversary of the Berkshire, Buckinghamshire and Oxfordshire Wildlife Trust (formerly known as the Berkshire, Buckinghamshire and Oxfordshire Naturalists' Trust or BBONT). A great deal has been achieved by the Trust in these 40 years, making this a fitting time to look back over its activities during this period.

It is a sad fact that many wildlife habitats have been, and are continuing to be, destroyed; so the Trust's role is essential in protecting local wildlife habitats and in encouraging people to learn about and enjoy our unique wildlife heritage. In the last few decades the Trust has saved 390 hectares of ancient woodland, 85 hectares of prime downland, 14 wetland sites and lakes, 15 old flower meadows and 83 hectares of woodland.

This could not have been achieved without the Local Wildlife Trust's members and volunteers who today number 12,500 and 1500 respectively. However, when the Trust was launched 40 years ago, only a small minority understood the implications of the widespread disregard and neglect of wildlife and the countryside. The inaugural meeting was held in Oxford in November 1959 and in the early days the Trusts' members and activists were largely people with a scientific background: botanists, zoologists, writers and academics specialising in all aspects of wildlife and conservation.

By the end of the 1960s the Trust had acquired 37 nature reserves, however, it was still the same elite few who took an interest in nature conservation and membership stood at only 1,850. The need to popularise its image and recruit supporters from a broader background was soon recognised, and in 1969 the Trust held its first sponsored walk; this became an annual event that now raises approximately £30,000 and involves hundreds of walkers. Throughout the 70s and 80s many fund-raising events were held at Oxford Town Hall and it seems that all the best known personalities in the wildlife world gave their time to be guest speaker: Johnny Morris, Sir Peter Scott, David Bellamy, Gerald Durrell and Sir David Attenborough.

The Thames Counties Appeal, launched in 1975 in conjunction with the World Wildlife Fund, was extremely

Left: *Notification of the inaugural meeting which took place in November 1959.* **Below:** *The sponsored flock.* **Bottom:** *Volunteers hard at work at the Warburg Reserve, Bix Bottom near Henley.*

successful; two years later £108,700 had been raised, which enabled the purchase of two important reserves at Hartslock, near Goring and Foxholes in north west Oxford, and the building of the Warden's house and information centre at Warburg Reserve near Henley.

Meanwhile the Trust has set up its first central office in Iffley, a converted loft next to the home of Michael Low, the Honorary Secretary at the time. A small room off Iffley Church Hall was also leased, and eight years later the trust moved to offices on Church Cowley Road.

The need to manage its grassland reserves led to the Trust buying a flock of hardy rare breed sheep, and to fund this, the somewhat eccentric Sponsored Sheep Scheme was launched. The scheme received national publicity and within weeks every sheep was sponsored. The sponsored sheep made an appearance on Blue Peter, outside the Houses of Parliament and for some years had their own annual open day for sponsors.

In November 1998 the Trust moved to larger premises in Armstrong Road, Littlemore, where a demonstration garden is being created and which is also a base for the conservation volunteer teams. The Trust now works to protect wildlife in many ways. Many readers will be familiar with its work in looking after its 90 nature reserves across the three counties. These sites are often the last

remaining havens for rare or endangered species, and half have been designated as a Site of Special Scientific Interest. The Trust's reserves are very diverse in character. Some are peaceful retreats, such as Iffley Meadows, an ancient wet meadowland in Oxford, famous for its snake's head fritillary flowers. These meadows are one of the few remaining places in Britain where this plant can be seen flowering in its natural surroundings. Since the Trust took over the management of the site there has been a welcome increase in the number of flowers.

Youngsters, on the other hand, may find the CS Lewis Reserve more fun. Bought by the Trust in 1969 it consists of a large pond surrounded by mixed woodland. The reserve lies behind what used to be the home of CS Lewis - author of the classic children's book 'The Lion, the Witch and the Wardrobe'. He used to walk in the woods with his friend JR Tolkein - and it is here that they dreamed up the fantasy worlds of Narnia and Middle Earth.

Although much good work has been carried out, the wildlife of the three counties remains under pressure, with species still being lost and many more on the brink of extinction. The role of the Berkshire, Buckinghamshire and Oxfordshire Wildlife Trust is as vital as ever, and staff and volunteers will continue the work of the Trust into the next millennium, providing a voice and a helping hand for local wildlife.

The Trust is entirely dependent on the support of local people and offers free to new members a guide to 90 of its nature reserves. To join simply phone 01865 775476 or e-mail the Trust at bbowt.cix.co.uk or visit the website www.wildlifetrust.org.uk/berksbucksoxon.

Top: *CS Lewis Reserve.*
Above left: *The Snake's Head Fritillary.*

On the ball where finance is concerned

Imagine, if you will, a cold February dawn at a spot far away from civilised Oxford: Aberdeen Docks. A ship is being loaded with goods bound for a North Sea oil rig. Suddenly two men walk boldly forward and demand that the dockers unload one of the containers. They are met with glares and mutterings, but the burly dockers do as they are told; cabbages, loaves, meat, cooking oils and all manner of other groceries are laid out, spreading right across the quayside in the freezing cold early morning air. The two brave men count everything methodically, then, having checked their documentation, they nod briefly, smile at the furious dockers, and beat a hasty retreat.

Readers who thought accountancy meant pen-pushers sitting in warm offices will be surprised to learn that the heroes of this little episode were Stephen Knowles and Simon Gibbs, who have since become partners of Edmund Gibbs, Accountants, of St Giles. They were engaged in investigating a suspected fraud; and although this is perhaps not one of the incidents in their career which they look back upon with the greatest pleasure, it nonetheless serves to demonstrate that there is more to accountancy than meets the eye.

Established in Oxford for over half a century, Edmund Gibbs has built up a reputation for combining friendliness with thoroughness and attention to detail, providing a flexible, professional and up-to-date service - whether pursuing fraudsters or helping clients plan their retirement! Many current clients have been with the firm since its very early days. The founder, Mr Edmund Gibbs, was the son of a well-known Oxford man, an eminent mathematician and a City Councillor. Edmund attended the old Bedford House and City of Oxford High Schools; he held a variety of high-ranking appointments during the war, ultimately reporting directly to the Financial Secretary to the British Government, and qualified as certified accountant in 1942. On his return to civilian life he worked briefly with Thornton & Thornton to gain experience in commercial and taxation matters before setting up his own practice. Many fellow ex-servicemen who had returned to found businesses in the city gravitated to 11 St Michael's Street, where Edmund practised from his late father's study. Edmund's wife Olive, formerly librarian at the City libraries, became receptionist, secretary and bookkeeper, and University landlady outside office hours, thereby supplementing the income from the practice.

The first couple of years were fraught with difficulty. The practice was refused an overdraft by the Bank on the grounds that Oxford did not need any more accountants. It was then turfed out of its home by Brasenose College, owners of the freehold, who classed it as a residential property. So Edmund moved to 15 Broad Street; and during his third year in practice he was appointed Company Secretary to the Headington United Football Club Company Limited, then an amateur club in the Spartan League. Thus began a 25-year association which brought great benefit to both parties; Headington United went on to become Oxford United, and the resultant publicity brought many new clients along to Edmund Gibbs.

From 1950 onwards the practice grew, and successive moves took it to 15 Broad Street (now Lloyds Bank), 14/15 Magdalen Street, 17 St Michael's Street, and finally, on 4th February 1963, to its present home at 46 St Giles.

Edmund Gibbs retired in 1984 after a very distinguished career. He was appointed City Councillor, Chairman of numerous committees and of the Southern Sport Council; he served as magistrate, and on the Council of the Chartered Association of Certified Accountants, becoming National President in 1978. His wife, not to be outdone, became the first woman Sheriff of Oxford,

Above: *Edmund Gibbs, founder of the company.*

Edmund Gibbs' merger with Frank G Ashworth & Co at Langdale Gate, Witney, in 1988. David Rickwood was admitted to partnership in 1995, on Frank Ashworth's subsequent retirement.

The firm currently has offices at St Giles and at Langdale Gate which provide the full range of traditional accountancy and taxation services for both corporate and private clients. In addition, its associated company, Edmund Gibbs Financial Services in Witney, offers all manner of financial services to help medium-sized, owner-managed businesses improve their financial performance; this includes advice on raising finance, retirement planning, savings plans, inheritance tax planning, or indeed any aspect of finance relevant to the client's individual circumstances. At the time of writing plans are being made to open a specialist 'payroll shop', also in Witney; both businesses will operate with a 'shop front' far removed from the sole practitioner's office of 1947. But although methods may have changed, the aims of the practice are the same today as they were then and will be in 2047: to use its expertise to the client's advantage, and to bring him, or her, peace of mind and security.

Lord Mayor of the City, Chairman of the County Council and was awarded the honorary Freedom of the City in 1982. At the time of his retirement, the practice had around 1,900 clients and six partners: Charles Cockings, the first Partner, had retired in 1978; Geoffrey French and Norman Cummings became partners in the early 60s, followed by Andrew Adams in 1971, Stephen Knowles in 1979 and Edmund's son, Simon Gibbs, who had joined the firm the previous year, in 1980. Stephen Wetherall was admitted as a partner in 1984, and more recently Frank Ashworth became a partner following

Above left: *46 St Giles, the firm's home.*
Top: *Edmund Gibbs, pictured in 1979.*

Accountants from copperplate to the computer age

Wenn Townsend, Chartered Accountants, a long established business in Oxford, is at the very forefront of 21st century audit and accounting technology and methodology. There is however more to this company than what some might regard as dry accounting procedures - there is a breadth of history and personal flavour, not often found in companies of this size.

Wenn Townsend started life in 1876 when Arthur Preston started to practise in High Street, Abingdon. He was a founder member of the Institute of Chartered Accountants in 1880. JHH Wenn joined him as an articled clerk in the early 1880s and qualified in 1887. By 1885 the business had moved to the premises at 55 Cornmarket Street, which it continued to occupy until 1957. Mr Preston, a well-known local personality, retired ultimately from the firm in 1908, although his commitment to public service actually belied that term 'retirement' somewhat - a three-year term as Mayor of Abingdon being just one small part of his post-accounting career. Joseph Wenn, in partnership with John Elsom, a fellow articled clerk of his with Arthur Preston, took over the partnership in 1908 when Preston retired. John Elsom retired in 1920 at which point Ernest White became a partner of Joseph Wenn. Ernest White was a key figure in the firm, having joined in 1891 and was managing clerk by 1910.

JHH Wenn, whose name lives on in the present company title, died in 1933, having been at his desk only the week before. James Townsend, the Townsend of the current business name, became a partner in 1947, after a period of working alone in Reading and later Oxford, although he sadly died just a year later. Townsend had coincidentally started his professional life with Joseph Wenn in 1909.

Harold Gray joined the firm as an articled clerk of Ernest White in January 1925 and took over the firm in partnership with Graham Watson on White's retirement in 1947. They remained partners until 1974 and acted as consultants long after that. Harold Gray in particular had close connections with the business for many years. He used to speak of the outbreak of war and the drama when the entire contingent of male staff from the Cornmarket Street office trooped enmasse to the recruitment station and joined up. Mr White, practitioner at the time, was having none of that, and later the same day went down himself and successfully de-registered them all! Harold Gray's son, son, Peter, who joined the firm in 1953, recalls fondly the days when the main considerations when attending audit were that you had to choose one of the necessary three colours of ink - green, red and purple - and that there was sufficient milk for the tea!

In 1957 the Oxford premises became inadequate for the burgeoning practice and the partners relocated to a former public house in St. Giles. The practice at Abingdon was re-established during the last war, and at the present time there are in all three separate practices covering Oxford, the main seat

Above left: *Ernest White in 1935.*
Below: *An early letter sent by the firm in 1914.*

```
                                        17th May 1912

Sir,

    We beg to apply for the post of Auditors to the Radcliffe
Infirmary and County Hospital.

    We have inspected the books and accounts and having regard
to the character of the Institution we should be prepared to undertake
the work for a fee of Fifteen Guineas per annum.

            Yours faithfully

            Wenn Elsom


Capt. Read
Radcliffe Infirmary
```

of the business, Abingdon, and Cirencester. Clients range from the self-employed to large private sector companies. The company describes its aim as providing quality, commitment and a timely service through working closely with clients to provide practical solutions to meet the client's needs. They can offer expert help in many areas including, among others, company formation, acquisitions, secretarial services, audit planning and computerisation.

And this helpfulness isn't just a service for the client. Wenn Townsend also aims to be a friendly and helpful employer, encouraging those wishing to arrange social functions - regular events include sporting activities and quizzes. So banish all those accounting stereotypes please! These people know how to have a good time when they're not working hard on their clients' behalf.

Wenn Townsend is the longest established accounting practice in Oxford, and Mr Gray, in his capacity as consultant, must surely have been one of the longest serving practitioners. It possibly indicates the kind of firm this is that anyone would choose to continue to work there long after official retirement age! The combined service of Ernest White and Harold Gray of over 100 years at Wenn Townsend clearly provided a secure structure of a flourishing business.

> *Clients range from the self-employed to large private sector companies*

The firm continues to look forward, and to meet the challenges of modern day accounting. Having embraced computerisation as a time-saving, efficiency-promoting notion, it is now used on a large scale to minimise paperwork, leaving more time to interact with the client. The personal touch is vital in retaining good customer relations and in ascertaining accurately client needs. Going from strength to strength is a feature of Wenn Townsend's history, and with the highest calibre of accountancy staff, regular training and specialist departments in tax, company law and employment, there seems to be little doubt that it will be a mark of the company's future as well.

Below: *The firm in the 1990s.*

May 6th 1935 saw the Silver Jubilee of King George V and Queen Mary. There are fancy hats in abundance as everyone settles down to the message of this particular day - enjoyment.

Acknowledgments

Many thanks to Oxfordshire County Council Photographic Archive for the loan of the images shown in the editorial section of this book.

The images on pages 10/11 (bigger picture), 12, 14/15, 16/17, 27,28,29,30/31,64, 78/79 courtesy of Oxfordshire County Council Photographic Archive/Newsquest (Oxfordshire Limited)

The images on pages 7 & 13 courtesy of Oxfordshire County Council Photographic Archive/BR/OPC

Dr Malcolm Graham, Head of Oxfordshire Studies, Centre for Oxfordshire Studies

Thanks are also due to
Peter Thomas who penned the editorial text and
Ann Ramsdale for her copywriting skills